ARTHUR ASHE

ARTHUR ASHE

A Biography

Richard Steins

GREENWOOD BIOGRAPHIES

GREENWOOD PRESS
WESTPORT, CONNECTICUT · LONDON

Library of Congress Cataloging-in-Publication Data

Steins, Richard.
 Arthur Ashe : a biography / Richard Steins.
  p. cm. — (Greenwood biographies, ISSN 1540–4900)
 Includes bibliographical references and index.
 ISBN 0–313–33299–1
 1. Ashe, Arthur. 2. Tennis players—United States—Biography.
3. African American tennis players—Biography. I. Title. II. Series.
GV994.A7S74 2005
796.342'092—dc22   2005016822

British Library Cataloguing in Publication Data is available.

Library of Congress Catalog Card Number: 2005016822
ISBN: 0–313–33299–1
ISSN: 1540–4900

First published in 2005

Greenwood Press, 88 Post Road West, Westport, CT 06881
An imprint of Greenwood Publishing Group, Inc.
www.greenwood.com

Printed in the United States of America

The paper used in this book complies with the
Permanent Paper Standard issued by the National
Information Standards Organization (Z39.48–1984).

10 9 8 7 6 5 4 3 2 1

Dedicated to the memory of Herman Steins
(1908–2004)

Success is a journey, not an outcome. The doing is often more important than the outcome.

—Arthur Ashe

CONTENTS

CONTENTS

Photo essay follows page 52

SERIES FOREWORD

In response to high school and public library needs, Greenwood developed this distinguished series of full-length biographies specifically for student use. Prepared by field experts and professionals, these engaging biographies are tailored for high school students who need challenging yet accessible biographies. Ideal for secondary school assignments, the length, format and subject areas are designed to meet educators' requirements and students' interests.

Greenwood offers an extensive selection of biographies spanning all curriculum related subject areas including social studies, the sciences, literature and the arts, history and politics, as well as popular culture, covering public figures and famous personalities from all time periods and backgrounds, both historic and contemporary, who have made an impact on American and/or world culture. Greenwood biographies were chosen based on comprehensive feedback from librarians and educators. Consideration was given to both curriculum relevance and inherent interest. The result is an intriguing mix of the well known and the unexpected, the saints and sinners from long-ago history and contemporary pop culture. Readers will find a wide array of subject choices from fascinating crime figures like Al Capone to inspiring pioneers like Margaret Mead, from the greatest minds of our time like Stephen Hawking to the most amazing success stories of our day like J. K. Rowling.

While the emphasis is on fact, not glorification, the books are meant to be fun to read. Each volume provides in-depth information about the subject's life from birth through childhood, the teen years, and adulthood.

A thorough account relates family background and education, traces personal and professional influences, and explores struggles, accomplishments, and contributions. A timeline highlights the most significant life events against a historical perspective. Bibliographies supplement the reference value of each volume.

INTRODUCTION

Arthur Ashe was a great American tennis player and a great champion of human rights, at home in the United States and around the world. As a tennis star, he was something of a surprise. An African American, he came from a family that was not wealthy. Through discipline and hard work he came to excel in a sport that traditionally had been dominated by well-to-do white people. He himself would have been the first to admit that he was not the most powerful player in the game, nor in the course of his career did he win a large number of top trophies. What he did have was a game that was graceful and relied as much on skill and strategy as on physical power to overwhelm his opponents. Since the time he played—the 1960s and 1970s—many new male players have come forward who play a game that has become dominated by power, especially by great muscular serves that propel the ball across the net at more than 100 miles per hour. Many of these younger players also have oversized egos and often get into arguments and heated displays of temper on the court.

Ashe was a kind of throwback to an earlier age of tennis. He was, above all, unfailingly polite and well mannered on the court, even if the referees made calls against him. He never would have thought of smashing his racket to the ground in anger, or of arguing with a linesman who made a call he disagreed with. That was not how his father had taught him to act. Arthur Ashe was a gentleman, and what other people thought of him mattered very much, not only on the tennis court but in all aspects of his life.

Ashe was a tennis player who bridged the gap between an older era and a new age in the sport. Most prominently, he was one of the first

African American men to reach the top of the tennis world. He learned to play tennis on the public courts of Richmond, Virginia, his home town—the same Richmond that had been the capital of the Confederacy during the Civil War in the early 1860s and was a center of black slavery, and the Richmond that in 1943, the year of Arthur's birth, was a segregated city. Even after young Arthur's talents were obvious for all to see, he was often kept from playing on most tennis courts in the South because he was black. The humiliation of segregation did not prevent him from developing his talent, and, in some way, it planted a seed that would lead him at a later time to oppose one of the great injustices of the world—apartheid, South Africa's oppressive system of racial segregation. And at the very end of his life, he would take up the cause of Haitian refugees who had been risking their lives to travel on flimsy boats to the freedom of the United States. By this time, the mature Arthur Ashe was willing to be arrested for demonstrating for the causes he believed in, to stand up and be counted as a voice against oppression, even if in so doing he risked offending others.

His interests in injustice abroad did not mean that he forgot the needs of African Americans in his own country. In the years after his tennis career ended, Ashe devoted countless hours and much of his own money supporting programs—many of which he founded—that were designed to improve the educational performance of young African American athletes. His interest in educational matters led him also to become the author of a major study of the history of African American athletes. And he used his ties to business—he had majored in business in college and, like many athletes, had connections to the business community through sponsorship of products—to pursue the social causes that he believed were important. While a board member of the insurance giant Aetna, Ashe became a passionate spokesman for improved health care for all Americans.

But Arthur Ashe's final challenge in life turned out not to be racial discrimination at home or his tennis opponents or human rights violations around the globe. The world was shocked when Ashe, an athlete in superb physical condition, suffered a heart attack at the age of 36. He underwent bypass surgery, but in 1983, he suffered another attack and was required to undergo yet another surgery. During this second surgery, Arthur Ashe was given a blood transfusion contaminated with the human immunodeficiency virus (HIV). This is the virus that causes the deadly disease known as AIDS (acquired immunodeficiency syndrome). Today, all blood used in transfusions is tested for HIV before being given to a patient. But back then, such a test did not exist, and because of one unfortunate moment of bad luck, Arthur Ashe contracted AIDS. The disease ravages and finally destroys its victims' immune systems, making them susceptible to all forms of infections.

Arthur wanted to keep his physical condition private. By the 1980s, he was a married man with a child, and he believed that his physical problems were no one's business but his own. Eventually, however, the news got into the hands of a newspaper, which told Ashe that it would tell the world he had AIDS. Ashe decided to go public at a press conference before the news appeared in the press—a loss of privacy that caused him and his family great pain.

Ashe decided to make the best of this unexpected turn of events. He began a campaign of public awareness about AIDS, speaking out about the disease and setting up a foundation to raise funds for use in the struggle against it. In doing so, Ashe performed a valuable public service. AIDS in the early 1990s carried a stigma with it. It was widely regarded as a disease of gay men who had contracted it during sex, or of people who were drug addicts who caught the illness by using dirty needles to shoot up their drugs. Ashe was a voice that helped the American people understand that AIDS could be contracted by anyone, that is was not limited only to gay men. AIDS did not discriminate. It affected men and women, adults and children, and people of all colors.

There was no way of knowing on the day of that press conference—April 8, 1992—that Ashe had less than a year to live. Those final months were filled with living—with his wife and child, protesting against apartheid and for the rights of Haitian refugees, and speaking out about AIDS. But in the end, the disease took him. On February 6, 1993, Arthur Ashe died at the age of 49 of AIDS-related pneumonia. He was mourned throughout the world. People remembered not only the graceful tennis champion, the gentle but committed fighter for human rights, but also the courageous young man who helped the people of the world understand a frightening disease.

Today, on Monument Avenue in Richmond stands a statue erected in memory of Arthur Ashe. It was a struggle, however, to get it built. Monument Avenue contains many statues devoted to the heroes of the Confederacy—generals like Robert E. Lee, who did everything in his power to preserve his beloved state of Virginia and its system of slavery. Arthur Ashe now stands along this avenue, a different kind of hero and a modern man who was also a son of the modern South, taking his place beside men of the old South. In many ways he represents America's—and tennis's—passage into the contemporary world, a world that he helped create.

Arthur Ashe lived a life filled with achievement. He reached the heights in the sport of tennis, only to be stricken at an early age by ill health. Yet through it all, he remained a courageous, dignified, and consistent person, someone who always knew who he was and what he stood for. This book will trace his life from its humble beginnings in Richmond to today. Years after his passing, Arthur Ashe remains a beloved athlete, a man who is rightly remembered and revered as an example of the best that America has to offer.

TIMELINE

1943 (10 July)	Arthur Ashe Jr. is born in Richmond, Virginia, the first son of Arthur Ashe Sr. and Mattie Cordell Cunningham Ashe.
1950	Arthur's mother dies during surgery, at the age of 27.
1953	Meets Ron Charity, a black tennis player and coach, who becomes his first teacher and mentor.
1957	Becomes the first African American to play in the Maryland boys' championships, his first integrated event.
1960	Moves to St. Louis, Missouri, to take coaching under Richard Hudlin and to complete his high school education.
1961	Enters UCLA, which has a first-rate tennis program.
1963	Arthur becomes the first African American player named to the Davis Cup team. He plays Davis Cup tennis intermittently between 1963 and 1978.
1965	Wins the NCAA men's singles championship, leading UCLA to the team title.
1963–1966	Serves in the U.S. Army, mainly at West Point, but continues to play in tennis matches.
1966	Graduates from UCLA.
1968	Wins the first U.S. Open title, his first Grand Slam singles title.

1970	Wins the Australian Open, his second Grand Slam title.
1970	Protests South Africa's system of apartheid. Requests that South Africa be expelled from the ILTA and is denied a visa to play in South Africa.
1973	Is granted a visa by South Africa and becomes the first black professional tennis player to play in South Africa's national championships.
1975	Wins Wimbledon crown, defeating Jimmy Connors. His third Grand Slam title.
1977	Marries Jeanne Moutoussamy, a photographer. Rev. Andrew Young, U.S. ambassador to the United Nations, performs the ceremony.
1979	Suffers first heart attack and undergoes quadruple bypass surgery.
1980	Formally retires from active tennis play.
1980–1985	Serves as captain of U.S. Davis Cup team. Team wins Davis Cups in 1981 and 1982.
1983	Undergoes second heart bypass surgery. Receives blood transfusion following surgery and contracts AIDS from tainted blood.
1985	Arthur is inducted into the Tennis Hall of Fame.
1985	Is arrested outside South African embassy in Washington while taking part in antiapartheid demonstration.
1986	Arthur and Jeanne adopt a baby girl and name her Camera.
1988	Is diagnosed with AIDS after coming down with a rare bacterial infection of the brain.
1988	Publishes A Hard Road to Glory, a monumental three-volume history of the African American athlete.
1991	Returns to South Africa as part of a delegation to observe political changes in the country.
1992	Reveals to the public that he is suffering from AIDS, after learning that his condition was about to be revealed by USA Today.
1992	Is arrested outside the White House while protesting the Bush administration's policy toward Haitian refugees.

1992	Addresses the United Nations on World AIDS Day, asking delegates to increase funding for AIDS research.
1992	Founds Arthur Ashe Foundation for the defeat of AIDS.
1993 (6 February)	Dies of AIDS-related pneumonia in New York at the age of 49.

Chapter 1

RICHMOND: THE EARLY YEARS

Richmond, the capital of Virginia, sweltered in the summer heat. The year 1943 was unusually hot and humid, and the city was gripped by a severe drought. Water was in short supply, and in these days before the widespread use of air-conditioning, the people suffered.

But the citizens of Richmond had other things on their mind in the summer of 1943. The nation was in the second year of war—World War II, which had started for the United States when the Japanese attacked Pearl Harbor, Hawaii, on December 7, 1941. By this time, the conflict was being fought across the globe, on the Atlantic Ocean, in North Africa, and on the island chains that stretched across the vast Pacific Ocean. Richmond had known war before. As the capital of the Confederate States of America (1861–1865), it had been the focal point and center of power of the rebellion of the Southern slave states against the government of the United States. When the Union armies of General Ulysses S. Grant approached the city in April 1865, the Confederate government collapsed and fled southward. As they fled the city, the Confederate troops set Richmond ablaze. Flames and smoke shot into the air, and from miles around, people could see the great city's destruction. Union soldiers entered the smoldering and abandoned ruins a day later, and President Abraham Lincoln walked the streets of the shattered city as weeping former slaves surrounded the president and thanked him for their freedom.

By 1943, the Civil War was nearly 80 years in the past. The city had been rebuilt, and although there were numerous monuments that honored the war dead and the sacrifices of those years, the actual physical scars of that conflict were no longer visible. When America entered

World War II in 1941, the citizens of Richmond, like other Americans, sent their sons into combat. Mothers, sisters, girlfriends, and wives stayed behind and worked the jobs men had previously held in factories. To save money, they tended their so-called victory gardens, where they grew vegetables that were harvested and cooked at home. The economic depression that had devastated the United States in the 1930s was over. Peacetime industries now switched to making war goods. Instead of producing dresses and shirts, clothing manufacturers now made uniforms for the army, navy, and marines. Factories that had made automobiles or auto parts now turned out jeeps, tanks, or other implements of war. Almost everyone who wanted to work found a job. Richmond, like other cities across the United States, hummed with activity as the country's economy sprang back to life and geared up for winning the war.

The population of Richmond in 1943 was about 193,000 people. Some 130,000 were white, while more than 60,000 of its citizens were African Americans, the descendants of the slaves who had been freed legally by the Civil War. Although slavery had long since been gone, as late as the 1940s there were still, in fact, two Richmonds—one white, the other black. The Civil War was over, and a modern city had emerged from the ashes of that terrible conflict. For African Americans, however, the legacy of the Civil War was a daily presence, a reminder of the many things that had not changed at all. That reality was summed up in one word: segregation—the enforced separation of whites and African Americans in almost all aspects of life. Black people lived in a segregated world in Richmond and elsewhere across the South. They lived in segregated housing, went to segregated schools and churches, were forced to use separate public restrooms, and were made to ride in the back of buses, while white people sat separately in the front. Most African Americans were not allowed to vote. They could not eat in most restaurants that catered to whites. In movie houses, they were required to sit separately in the balcony. And they could not play at public playgrounds that were reserved for whites. Blacks traveling through Richmond, or anywhere else in the South, could not stay at hotels that were for whites only—and there were few hotels anywhere for blacks. Instead, they would stay at the homes of relatives, friends, or people who were simply kind enough to take in African American travelers. The world black people lived in was dangerous and potentially violent, and anyone who dared not to follow the practices of segregation or who attempted to challenge the system that kept African Americans "in their place" might face violence or even death.[1]

In Richmond, and throughout the South, World War II had almost no effect on segregation, which had been in place since the end of the

Civil War and the abolition of slavery in 1865. Segregation, in fact, was a product of peace. When the Northern occupation troops were pulled out of the South in 1877 as part of a deal that gave the presidential election of 1876 to Rutherford B. Hayes of Ohio, the day-to-day running of local government in the South was returned to white people. When Northern troops occupied the South, many blacks had participated in government, and some had even been elected to the U.S. Congress. Over the next two decades, however, white-run governments across the South enacted segregation laws to separate the races and to guarantee white control. Blacks were gradually excluded from politics and were robbed of the liberties that they had supposedly won as a result of the Civil War. Segregation laws were still in effect in the 1940s. Some states had more severe segregation policies than others, but all Southern states had them.

Nevertheless, despite the oppression that kept them second-class citizens without civil rights, blacks had expressed their patriotism for their country and gone off to war, as did whites, serving with distinction in what were still-segregated armed forces. Men were drafted into the armed forces, or they enlisted. Blacks fought courageously in all-black units, which were commanded by white officers. The also worked behind the battle lines in all-black noncombatant units, driving trucks, maintaining equipment, and doing the countless tasks required to support the millions of Americans in uniform. An all-black unit of aviators, called the Tuskegee Airmen, achieved worldwide fame for their heroism as combat fighter pilots.

African Americans believed that their service and sacrifices for their country in World War II entitled them—at long last—to the equality they had been denied. Many hoped that the war would bring an end to segregation. In 1943, however, those hopes were still a distant dream, and the official, legal end of segregation would not come for another twenty years with the passage of the Civil Rights Act of 1964 and the Voting Rights Act of 1965. In the meantime, the people of Richmond—both white and black—labored in the war effort, hoping to bring victory to the United States and its allies.

THE ASHE FAMILY

On July 10, 1943, in the midst of this steamy, wartime summer in Richmond, Arthur Robert Ashe and Mattie Cordell Cunningham, a young African American couple who had married in 1938, gave birth to their first son. They named him Arthur Robert Ashe Jr. The baby was born in St. Phillip's Hospital, a segregated facility for blacks only.

Arthur Sr., the proud father, had grown up near South Hill, Virginia. His father, Edward "Pink" Ashe (who, according to family tradition, was probably called "Pink" because of his light complexion, although the origin of the nickname is not certain) had been born in North Carolina in 1873. Pink married Amelia Johnson (known in the family as "Ma") and settled in South Hill. Unfortunately, Pink deserted his family in the 1920s, when Arthur Sr. was a young boy. The youngster was left to care for his family, and perhaps these premature and grave responsibilities accounted for his seriousness as an adult. The Ashes could trace their ancestry back to the early 1700s, when slaves were brought from Africa to work on the farms, in the homes, and, later, on plantations in the British colony of Virginia. The Ashe ancestors were slaves who had been owned by Governor Samuel Ashe of Virginia. Like many slaves in the colonial period, they adopted the name of their owner. Thus the name "Ashe" was passed down to generations into the twentieth century.

Mattie Cordell Cunningham, Arthur Jr.'s mother, was the child of Johnnie and Jimmie (nicknamed "Big Mama") Cunningham of Oglethorpe, Georgia. They had migrated to Westwood, a black neighborhood west of Richmond, in the 1920s. Johnnie and Big Mama had 10 children. In 1932, Johnnie died, leaving Big Mama to raise her large family all on her own. She was not wealthy, but Big Mama had a generous heart and was always willing to share whatever she had with her family. When Mattie and Arthur Sr. were married, they lived in her house for a time until they were able to save some money for a move to Richmond in search of work and a better life as well as a home of their own.

Arthur Sr. was willing to do almost any kind of work after they settled in the Virginia capital. In his young life he took jobs as a chauffeur and handyman, and he learned carpentry. By all accounts an honorable, moral, and upright man, Arthur Sr. believed in the importance of hard work and of adhering to the highest moral code of behavior. He was also a religious man who went to church every Sunday and expected his children to go to church too. Arthur Sr. was, using familiar language, a "strict" father. His son Arthur, and later Arthur's younger brother Johnnie, who was born in 1948, were expected to show respect for their elders. When they were young schoolboys, their father made very clear what was expected of them: they were to come home on time and do their homework and not hang out on street corners. And one of the most important lessons they were taught—one that would have a great impact on young Arthur's life—was to play by the rules, even if the rules at times seemed unfair. Playing by the rules and not making a fuss when things didn't always go your way was, according to Arthur's father, a way of guaranteeing that you would be around in the future to have another chance at achieving your goal.

It was a lesson that he had learned from the hard experience of segregation, which taught him that a low profile was often the safest way of staying alive. That did not mean that Arthur Sr. approved of segregation. He didn't. It was a one-sided set of rules that were unfair, unjust, and damaging. But in "playing" by them—which they had no choice but to do—blacks hoped to protect themselves from violence and other forms of retaliation. Arthur Jr. grew up in the civil rights era in America, when more and more blacks *did* challenge the rules of segregation. His father was not the kind of man who was on the front lines of the struggle, although he supported civil rights will all his heart. His basically conservative approach to life was something that Arthur absorbed early on and carried onto the tennis court.

Doing well in school was never a problem for Arthur. He loved school and always achieved the highest grades on his report cards—which was expected by his father. Arthur's brother Johnnie was different. Unlike Arthur, Johnnie was more rebellious and mischievous. He was more likely to get into trouble, while Arthur was always a good boy. Arthur's father often wondered why the boys were so different. Why couldn't Johnnie be more like Arthur? He later came to realize that Arthur was unusual and special, and that there was nothing really wrong with Johnnie. He was just more like other boys, a typical kid who sometimes got into trouble but was really a good boy. Strangely enough given his rebelliousness, when he grew up, Johnnie chose a career in the U.S. Marine Corps— a military organization that represents the height of strict discipline and obedience. Arthur and Johnnie were only five years apart, but there was no rivalry between the brothers that anyone can remember. As adults they even went into business together briefly. Whatever their differences in temperament, they were both brought up with the same standards and expectations from their parents, especially their father. Throughout their lives, they loved and supported each other, even as they followed very different career paths.

Moral uprightness and an unbending refusal to compromise on issues of morality and fairness: these were lessons that were deeply ingrained in young Arthur by both his father and his young mother. He would remember these lessons again and again—as a young child, as a teenager, as one of the world's most famous and successful athletes, and, in the final years of his life, as a middle-aged man facing an insurmountable health crisis.

Arthur Sr. also made sure that he instilled the importance of religion in the lives of his children. Young Arthur was first taken to his father's church, the First Presbyterian, on the corner of Monroe and Catherine Streets in Richmond. Arthur's mother, however, went to the Westwood Baptist Church in Westwood, and Arthur would also go to her church on different occasions. He would later be introduced to the Episcopal religion, and as a teenager had the opportunity to go to Roman Catholic masses. Throughout his life, Arthur always considered himself a Christian, but he did not identify strongly with one denomination over another.[2] He was a spiritual person who believed in a loving God and found himself comfortable with the message of religion, regardless of denomination.

In 1947, Arthur Ashe Sr. was offered a job with the city of Richmond. It was a true opportunity for advancement and more money, but it required him to move his family. Arthur Sr. accepted the position as a special police officer overseeing Brook Field, a segregated park that was for blacks only. On the grounds of the Brook Field was a small house that was meant for the use of the park officer, and Arthur, Mattie, and Arthur Jr. moved into it when Mr. Ashe began his duties. Brook Field was a park with trees and benches, but it also had a wide range of recreational facilities, including a swimming pool and tennis courts. Thus, his father's new job placed the young Arthur Ashe in the immediate vicinity of the game—tennis—that ultimately would change his life.

Sometime after their move to the house in Brook Field, young Arthur began wandering over to the tennis courts, where he watched black players—some young, some more mature—playing this game. He was soon able to get his hands on an inexpensive racket and quickly discovered that he really enjoyed swinging the racket and hitting balls. He knew nothing about the game of tennis, but he knew he liked the motion, the feel of hitting a ball against a wall, the pleasure of seeing people bigger than he was play this fascinating game. He had no way of knowing at the time that he was at the beginning of a remarkable journey that would take him to the top of the tennis world. This skinny little African American boy from segregated Richmond would become one of the world's great tennis players.

TENNIS: THE GAME AND THE WORLD IT WAS PLAYED IN

The Origins of Tennis

The game of tennis has been played in one form or another for many centuries. A game called *jeu de palme* ("game of the palm")—a kind of handball—played in France in the 1300s may have been one of the origins of modern tennis.

The version of tennis we see played today is a game where two players ("singles" tennis) or pairs of players ("doubles" tennis) hit a ball with a racket back and forth over a net. When a player misses hitting the ball or fails to hit a ball within the boundaries of the tennis court, the opponent is awarded points. A player can also receive points by hitting an "ace," a ball that lands on first bounce within a narrowly defined area of the tennis court.

Modern tennis began in Great Britain in the 1870s. It was called "lawn tennis" because it was played on grass courts by upper-class ladies and gentlemen. Tennis has, until recent times, been thought of as a sport for elite and well-to-do people. Early tennis players wore heavy clothing on the court. Women had on long skirts, petticoats, and corsets, while men wore sweaters and long, white flannel pants. The game had an aura of politeness and upper-class gentility about it: the players were gracious to each other, always shook hands after the match, and almost never challenged the call of linesmen (the referees who watched to make sure that the ball bounced properly within the bounds of the court). Displays of temper on the tennis court were unheard of.

Tennis can be played by anyone with any level of skill—as long as you can hit a ball back and forth over a net. Some people, in fact, may simply enjoy hitting the ball back and forth over the net and not bothering to keep score. The top professional players, however, are athletes who have great physical strength and the ability to hit precise, powerful shots in a game that requires both offensive and defensive moves. The great tennis players of today are major athletic stars. They endorse products, have fans and fan clubs, and earn millions of dollars in prize money. The major tennis stars of today—Venus and Serena Williams, Andre Agassi, and Andy Roddick, for example—are seen on TV and in newspapers and magazines and are known around the world. In addition to their skills in tennis, we know all about their private lives simply by watching TV.

The Rules of Tennis

The rules of tennis were first created at the All-England Croquet Club in Wimbledon, a town near London. In the 1870s, the club decided to set aside one of its lawns for the playing of tennis. (The club up to that time was dedicated to the playing of another lawn game known as croquet.) As the game became popular, the club changed its name to the All-England Croquet and Lawn Tennis Club, and in 1877, the club held its first tennis championship matches. The All-England club also decided that the tennis court would be a rectangle that was 78 feet long and 28 feet wide. And they created a scoring system that is unique to tennis. Under the point system, the player who wins a volley first gets 15 points. The score is then "15-love." In tennis, the word *love* means zero. If the other player wins the next volley, the score is then "15-all," meaning the players each have 15 points. If the first player wins the next volley, the score is then 30–15. If he wins the next point, score is then 40–15. If the opposing player wins the next two points, however, the score is then 40–all. In tennis, this situation is called "deuce." At deuce a player must win the next two volleys in order to win the game. In order to win a set, a player must win six games. To win the match, a player must win two or three sets, depending on the rules of the particular tournament. In women's professional tennis, two sets wins the match, while in men's tennis, three sets are usually required to win the match.

These rules have varied over time, and in some modern tournaments, they may not be exactly the same. But the point system, the dimensions of the court, and the general rules governing a match are followed by most tennis organizations.

The Spread of Tennis

The All-England club is still in existence, and the Wimbledon tennis championship is perhaps most prestigious trophy in all of tennis. The rules and dimensions of the court created in England in the 1870s were modified slightly over the years, and some confusion about the rules of the game occurred as the popularity of tennis spread to other countries. The first U.S. tennis championship was held in 1880 at the Staten Island Cricket and Baseball Club in New York. A woman named Mary Outerbridge is credited with buying some rackets and balls and giving them to her brother, who was the director of the Staten Island club. He was fascinated enough with the sport to hold a tournament. Interest in tennis grew in the United States, and in 1881, the U.S. National Lawn Tennis Association was created. It was later renamed the U.S. Lawn Tennis Association (USLTA) and in 1975, the name was changed to the U.S. Tennis Association (USTA).

In the 1880s and 1890s, tennis also became popular in France, Australia, and New Zealand. Many nations today have their own national championships, but the four most prestigious are the British (Wimbledon), and the U.S., French, and Australian tournaments. Any player—male or female—who wins all four of these tournaments in a season is said to have won the "Grand Slam" of tennis. There is no higher goal or honor among tennis players than to win the Grand Slam of tennis.

In the first half of the twentieth century, tennis did not have a mass following the way baseball did. Television changed all that. With the coverage of the Grand Slam events and other professional matches, tennis personalities emerged—people who were essentially created by TV and who, at times, acted as if they were TV stars. Although tennis has never developed the huge following that baseball or football has enjoyed, it nevertheless is seen by millions of people and has more followers and fans today than at any other time. Still, in the popular imagination, many people still regard it as an "elite" sport.

By the 1950s, tennis had been well established in the United States for some 80 years. The major players of the period were largely American, British, and Australian. Although it required equipment and a tennis court to play a real game, anyone—including kids—could swing a racket. And a racket, even a small, cheaply made one, could usually be found with ease, as could a ball.

A YOUNG BOY'S LOVE OF TENNIS

No one can explain what attracts a person to one sport over another. Nor can anyone say why some people excel in sports and others do not. Are athletes just born with their talent, or are they products of hard work, talent, and fierce dedication to succeed? Or some combination of both? Arthur Ashe was introduced to tennis by accident—the tennis courts he first played on were across the street from the house he lived in. But what attracted this young boy, whose family had no history of success in sports, to athletics in the first place? And to a sport that, in the 1940s and 1950s, was distinctly dominated and controlled by white people. White people financed tennis in their exclusive clubs, and white boys and girls played amateur and professional tennis. In the 1950s, the great female African American athlete Althea Gibson rose to the top of the women's tennis world, winning two singles championships at Wimbledon, in 1957 and 1958, but she was an exception. For young Arthur, there were no nationally known black men succeeding in the white world of tennis. But there was, in fact, another world of tennis—a world in which young African American boys and girls played tennis among themselves. In Richmond, there were black men who played tennis—and played well—and Arthur would soon meet them.

At the time Arthur began to show an interest in tennis, a terrible tragedy struck his family. His beloved mother died suddenly. Mattie had gone into the hospital for surgery, but because of an underlying heart disease, which no one was aware she had, she did not survive the operation.

She was only 27 years old. It was 1950, and Arthur was not yet seven years old. The loss of his mother was a devastating blow to him, his brother Johnnie, and, of course, his father. For the rest of his life, Arthur remembered vividly how his father had cried when he told them their mother was dead. Without a mother, Arthur became even more dependent on and attached to his father, who now had the responsibility of being a single parent with two young boys to raise. Luckily, the Ashe and Cunningham families were large, and Arthur grew up with many loving aunts and uncles and cousins. To help with household duties, Arthur Sr. hired an elderly woman, Mrs. Otis Berry. Mrs. Berry spent a lot of time with the boys. A religious woman, she took Arthur and his brother to St. James Episcopal Church in Richmond. For a time, Mrs. Berry was a kind of substitute mother, giving maternal care to Arthur and Johnnie in the first difficult years without their mother.

Arthur was also to discover that people in the world of black tennis cared about him and wanted him to succeed. The little boy who lived across the street from the park and who loved to swing a racket, it turned out, was also talented. The first black tennis player who noticed Arthur Ashe and spotted a potential talent was a man named Ronald Charity. Charity was an African American who loved to play tennis and was eager to promote the sport among young black men. He would often practice his swing alone on the courts at Brook Field, and he began to notice a kid who liked to hang around the tennis court watching older, experienced players. One day, Charity approached Arthur and asked him if he'd like to learn to play. In Arthur's words, "As casually as that, my life was transformed."[3]

Charity took it upon himself to give Arthur some early coaching, especially in the basic use of the racket. He coached and he encouraged, because he believed that the young man had the capacity to be a great tennis player. After a few years of careful coaching and supervised practice, Charity believed that Arthur was ready to compete in youth tournaments that were held among black players in Richmond. Coaching was one way to develop a tennis player's skills, but there was no substitute for what could be learned in a match: the talents of a real opponent, playing before other people, learning to have to live with calls that you felt were perhaps not right or even outright unfair, and—perhaps most important—learning to live with defeat as well as victory.

Charity used his influence to get Arthur into the Richmond Racquet Club, which was an organization for black tennis players in Richmond. He believed that Arthur's skills would be greatly enhanced by competing against older players. In 1953, when Arthur was 10 years old, Charity also was able to get him into a development program for young people in another black tennis organization, the American Tennis Association (ATA).

A WISE MENTOR

Arthur progressed brilliantly as a young tennis player. As he improved his skills, Ronald Charity eventually realized that the young man needed to move onto another level of training. He had done all he could, but now, with the permission of Arthur's father, Charity introduced the young player to Doctor Robert Walter Johnson of Lynchburg, Virginia. Dr. Johnson, an African American, was active in ATA tennis and had built tennis courts on the grounds of his home. Every summer, he would take in five or six talented young black players and run a kind of tennis training camp. One of his great successes had been Althea Gibson, who went on to enjoy an international career.

Dr. Johnson's personality was very much like Arthur's father's. He was highly disciplined, and he accepted no excuses for poor behavior or half-hearted effort. At the same time, he was fair and caring. In later years, Arthur wrote that Dr. Johnson "insisted that I be unfailingly polite on the court, unfalteringly calm and detached, so that whites could never accuse me of meanness. I learned well."[4] Only once did Arthur challenge Dr. Johnson. In his first year at the camp, Dr. Johnson told Arthur to do something a certain way. Arthur said no, Ron Charity had taught him to do it another way, and he saw no reason to change. Dr. Johnson immediately called Arthur's father and told him to come and pick up the boy—he was being asked to leave the camp. Dr. Johnson would not tolerate insubordination from anyone, least of all an unformed youngster who thought he knew best. Arthur Sr. arrived and told young Arthur in no uncertain terms that he was to do what Dr. Johnson said—period. No arguments, no discussion. Arthur, as usual, got the message, and he was allowed to remain at camp. His challenge to Dr. Johnson was uncharacteristic for him—he had been carefully taught, and he built on his learning from this particular lesson.

From 1953 until his graduation from high school, Arthur spent part of every summer at Dr. Johnson's camp in Lynchburg. The type of training he received there meshed well with the life he lived with his father: discipline, close attention to school work, obedience to adults, and tennis practice aimed at improving basic skills—technical as well as personal. These were the lessons that shaped his character as a young man and that translated on the tennis court as well to the kind of player he would become. Another lesson that shaped his character in these years was his first "back-of-the-bus" experience. Boarding a bus to Lynchburg, Arthur noticed that the seat directly behind the driver was vacant. It was a good seat, because it offered a great view of the countryside en route between Lynchburg and Richmond. At this point in his life, Arthur certainly knew that blacks were usually required to ride in the back of buses in the South. There might have been minor exceptions here and there, but for an African American, it was safest to assume that blacks had to ride in the back of the bus, regardless of where you were in the South. But in his excitement and enthusiasm, he had just forgotten this cardinal practice of segregation. The bus driver turned to him and, in a matter-of-fact voice, told him that he would not be allowed to sit in that seat. Arthur picked up his bag and moved to the back of the bus. He was always his father's son: he did not challenge this "call," even though it had gone against him. But he never forgot the sting of humiliation and hurt, the sheer injustice of being forced to sit in the rear of a bus simply because the shade of his skin was darker than a white person's.

What was Dr. Johnson's training like? For one, it was not all about tennis. Arthur and the other young people Dr. Johnson agreed to take on had to perform chores around the house, such as cleaning the doctor's dog kennel, doing garden work, and maintaining the tennis courts. Tennis instruction was given by Dr. Johnson and his son Robert in the morning. After lunch, the trainees practiced tennis and did their assigned chores. Food was healthful and plentiful—although the doctor did not provide sweets of any kind, because he believed they were detrimental to an athlete's development—and after a hearty dinner, trainees attended classroom sessions run by Dr. Johnson. Sometimes films were shown of tennis matches, and discussions were held about the film or the day's practice sessions. In other words, the training was aimed at developing the entire person, not just the tennis player. Dr. Johnson believed that a tennis champion needed to be a well-rounded, balanced, and disciplined person, and his total program was geared toward shaping such players.

The tennis training at Dr. Johnson's camp was heavily slanted toward drills. The students played very few matches with each other. Instead, they hit balls back and forth, sometimes for hours on end. Arthur recalled hitting backhands across the court for an hour without stopping. It seemed boring, but it was an essential way to develop a strong backhand—hitting a ball with the racket held in such a way that the back of the hand is facing the direction the ball is hit in. As a young boy, Arthur had first come to enjoy tennis simply by hitting a ball, sometimes for hours on end, so these kinds of drills were not necessarily something he found difficult to do.

EARLY TOURNAMENTS

Playing against an opponent—whether in an informal game or a tournament—is the lifeblood of any tennis player. All the solitary practice in the world, hitting balls against a wall or swinging a racket to strengthen your serve and arm muscles—is nothing compared with the challenge of a live—and unpredictable—opponent. For young Arthur, the main obstacle to his advancement into competitive play with other young African American players was his size and weight. But as he approached being a teenager, when an inevitable growth spurt would take place, Dr. Johnson enrolled him in an ATA competition for his age. That competition, in 1955, was the first of many that Arthur won in the boys' division. The years between 1955 and 1958 were important for Arthur's development as a tennis player and as a young man. Arthur almost always won, and the kind of tennis player he was, including the character traits he exhibited on the court when facing an opponent, was becoming more obvious. On the court, he was always a young gentleman. He played well, but, equally important, he acted well, always as a good sportsman whose character enhanced the game.

And these character traits impressed Dr. Johnson, who had a mission greater than simply training talented young African American players. He hoped to "break the color barrier" in tennis, meaning, he wanted more and more black players to be able to compete in previously whites-only tournaments. Thanks to his efforts, he was able to enter two of his trainees in a white tournament in Virginia in 1950, but they were not the most skillful players and they were defeated early in the tournament. Although disappointed, Johnson kept trying. He worked out an agreement with the USLTA in which he would hold a tournament among African American contenders each year to determine the best player. The USLTA, in turn, promised to hold open a few places in their tournament for young players for the best African American players from Dr. Johnson's tournaments.

This agreement was not perfect, but like so many other examples in the battle for civil rights for blacks during these years, it was a beginning, a foot in the door to white tournaments. Dr. Johnson was a wise man who understood that his best trainees had to be more than skilled tennis players. They also had to have the psychological strength to withstand what could be a stressful and even abusive transition of a black person into white tennis. The integration of professional baseball in the 1940s had been difficult, and Dr. Johnson learned from having observed that experience. One of the reasons that Jackie Robinson, the first black player to enter the major leagues, was chosen to play for the Brooklyn Dodgers was that he was believed to have the mental strength to withstand a grueling test. And he did. Although it seems almost impossible to believe from the perspective of professional sports today, Jackie Robinson's entry into professional "white-only" baseball was a highly charged, controversial moment. He was occasionally booed and even spat on by other players as he appeared on the field. But he did not react in kind. He never lost his temper. He just played superb baseball, and within a short period, he—and the other black players who followed him—were accepted into major-league baseball. Today, professional baseball is fully integrated and has on its teams not only African Americans but men from Caribbean countries and, more recently, some of the best players from Japan.

Dr. Johnson saw that Arthur Ashe not only was a potentially great tennis player but that he seemed to have a Jackie Robinson-like temperament. Perhaps young Arthur had the mental strength to face the abuse that might come his way as a pioneer in the breaking down of racial barriers in sports. But first, he would need to advance a step at a time.

NOTES

1. For an excellent description of Richmond during World War II, see Francis Earle Lutz, *Richmond in World War II* (Richmond, VA: Dietz Press, 1951), especially pp. 30–96. Although written before the end of segregation, the book covers the contributions of African Americans to the city during the period of U.S. participation in World War II (1941–1945).

2. Ashe, Arthur, and Arnold Rampersad, *Days of Grace: A Memoir* (New York: Ballantine, 1993), p. 316.

3. Ibid., p. 65.

4. Ibid., p. 128.

Chapter 2

GROWING UP
PLAYING TENNIS

For Dr. Johnson, a major goal was to get Arthur into a U.S. Lawn Tennis Association (USLTA) competition and to build his career opportunities on that event. The agreement he had worked out with the USLTA was easier to take advantage of outside the South; in Arthur's home city of Richmond, the racial barriers were slow to tumble. In 1958, Arthur was 15 years old, and the USLTA, even with its mixed record on race, ranked him among the top five amateur players nationally in his age bracket. But Arthur continually was refused admission to the Mid-Atlantic Championships, a Richmond tournament that had always been for whites only. The Mid-Atlantic turned him down again in 1959 in a stubborn refusal to drop racial barriers that were beginning to fall elsewhere in the United States, especially outside of the South. It was an infuriating and unfair situation: the USLTA could look at Arthur and clearly see that he was a talented, emerging tennis player, yet the national leadership of the organization was very slow to order its local affiliates to abolish racial barriers. Tennis, like so many other organizations in the United States during these years, was very conservative and afraid to make major changes.

One barrier in the South did give way in 1959. Arthur and another black player were invited to play in the Orange Bowl International Junior Cup, which was a competition sponsored by the USLTA that featured young players not only from the United States but from around the world. Even the timid USLTA was embarrassed to keep American blacks out of a tournament that invited players from foreign countries. Although he was beaten after his fourth match, Arthur had the opportunity to meet players from other countries and to play against older boys.

The years 1958 and 1959 were times of success and disappointment. Arthur played in mixed-race tournaments outside the South and usually won. In the fall of 1958 he entered the all-black Maggie Walker High School in Richmond and joined the tennis team. In his second and third years he won the black high school state tennis tournament. During these years, he was also beginning to develop a more mature level of skill. Although he remained an unusually thin player—he was thinner than the average male player—his serve in particular was becoming more powerful and accurate, and it would always be a hallmark of his game.

Because he was one of the top juniors in the ATA, Arthur was invited to enter the national amateurs' tournament at the West Side Tennis Club in Forest Hills, New York. Forest Hills was *the* American tennis shrine. It was the center of the American national tennis championships games that later became the prestigious U.S. Open. To play at Forest Hills, regardless of your age bracket, meant you had reached the top levels of tennis. In his first try in this tournament, Arthur was beaten by an Australian player, Rod Laver, who went on to be one of the greatest tennis champions in history. Still, it had been an honor to play on the courts of this distinguished tennis club.

Arthur's late teen years were characterized by stable, regular routines that revolved around school and tennis. In 1955, his father had remarried. Arthur's stepmother, Lorene Kimbrough, was a loving woman who had two children of her own from a previous marriage. His new "blended" family was a source of stability and strength when it was formed and, undoubtedly, during the personal and professional challenges that lay ahead of him.

By 1960, Dr. Johnson was still striving to get Arthur the opportunity to play into a tennis world beyond Richmond and the South. The constant frustration of tennis doors slammed in his face because he was black and the difficulties of simple travel throughout the South were signals that for a tennis player with the potential for a national reputation, Richmond had to be left behind. One way to avoid the racial discrimination in Richmond and other Southern cities was simply to play nationally in tournaments in which he would be accepted. The USLTA continued not to enforce any uniform policy regarding racial barriers, but Arthur could no longer be ignored.

For all the prejudice Arthur had experienced, Richmond was still his home, the location of his family and friends and the positive memories of his introduction to tennis. His father had built a house with his own hands in the town of Gum Springs, near Richmond, where he continued to live with Arthur's stepmother. It would be hard to leave, even for all the positive opportunities that lay ahead.

The plan to broaden his horizons and opportunities—fostered by Dr. Johnson with the approval of Arthur's father—involved moving to St. Louis, Missouri, and living in the home of Richard Hudlin, a respected African American tennis coach and high school teacher. Hudlin taught at an all-black school—which Arthur would attend in his final year of high school—and he lived in a predominantly black neighborhood. Nevertheless, St. Louis was not as rigidly segregated as most parts of the South. Although blacks and whites by and large lived in separate neighborhoods, public accommodations were not segregated and the rigid rules of the segregated South were not in force. This overall environment was far more positive.

In addition, as a coach, Hudlin pushed Arthur to new heights. He encouraged him, for example, to be more forceful in his game and not simply to hit balls from the back of the court but to rush the net and return his opponent's serve with aggressive skill. Rushing to the net can be a risky move. If a player rushes the net and catches the opponent's return, he or she can smash the ball with such power that the bounce becomes impossible for the opponent to return. On the other hand, an opponent can hit a ball to the back of the court while a player charges to the net. If the ball is within bounds, it will have sailed past and be impossible to return. Hudlin was very effective in teaching Arthur this essential tennis move, which he would have to master to play in the big leagues.

While in St. Louis, Arthur won his first national USLTA championship for his age group. In November of that year, he won the National Indoor Championship, a prestigious victory for the young player. Six months later, he returned to Virginia and was allowed to play in the USLTA-sponsored Interscholastic Tournament in Charlottesville. Arthur won, a victory that made Dr. Johnson particularly proud, since he had long dreamed of a black player taking that trophy. Arthur also continued to win in ATA events and enjoyed a growing reputation.

Now he was about to graduate from high school, and he needed to think about college. Obviously, the ability to continue to play tennis would be an important—the perhaps the most important—factor in his choice of a school. He did not have to think for long: the school came to him. The University of California at Los Angeles (UCLA) had an extensive tennis program that was considered one of the best in the country. Located in sunny Southern California, the school was an ideal place for year-round outdoor play. UCLA knew about Arthur Ashe, and they wanted him. To entice him, they offered Arthur a full, four-year scholarship. Other schools also offered scholarships, but Arthur had little trouble deciding on UCLA because of its superb reputation for intercollegiate tennis. It was also not far from another school that had a good tennis program, the University of Southern California (USC). USC would also field some of the best college tennis players, most of whom Arthur would meet in competition over the years that followed. In all, California provided an excellent environment for college tennis, and in the 1960s, it was from the ranks of college tennis that many of the great U.S. players were emerging. Many college freshmen experience living away from their parents for the first time when they are 18, but Arthur already had done this when he moved to St. Louis during his high school years. So he was prepared for the challenges of college life.

TENNIS IN COLLEGE

Once in college, Arthur had to decide on an academic major. Today, the top tennis stars make millions of dollars through their tournament play. When Arthur was coming up in the game, however, amateur tennis players made next to nothing. As a college student, he needed to think of a profession so he would be able to earn a living at some point after he had to stop playing the game—just like all athletes had to realize that as they got older, they would eventually have to stop playing the game, even though they would still be young in years. Arthur's first thought was that he would major in architecture. But J. D. Morgan, the tennis coach at UCLA, persuaded Arthur that architecture courses would leave him less time for playing and that a more practical major would help set him up for the years after he stopped playing tennis. Accordingly, Arthur decided to major in business administration, and it turned out to be a wise choice for the later years. Arthur would eventually be asked to serve on many company boards of directors not only because of his stature as a tennis player but because of his knowledge of the business world.

Going away to college should always be a broadening experience for any young person, because of the opportunity to meet new people from diverse backgrounds and to be exposed to a wider world beyond one's childhood. For Arthur, UCLA was such an experience. To begin with, he was increasingly on his own. His father was in touch by telephone, but Southern California was many more miles away from Virginia than was St. Louis. In addition, as he became a young adult, Arthur was called on to make many decisions without the day-to-day guidance his mentors and family had provided. The student body at UCLA was a mix not found in Arthur's Richmond or even in the school he attended in St. Louis. Arthur's first roommate was white and Jewish. And he had the opportunity to go on a few dates with Asian and white girls—a practice that could have led to abuse and even violence in the segregated South, where interracial relationships were scorned and could prove dangerous for the couples involved.

An old tennis friend from his teen years, Charlie Pasarell, who was a native of Puerto Rico, had also decided to go to UCLA, so his familiar face was a connection with the immediate past. Arthur decided to join a black fraternity, Kappa Alpha Psi, although other, nonblack fraternities had accepted him. He felt comfortable with white students, but he also believed he should support an all-black fraternity and perhaps give support to other African American students who may not have been so self-assured. His main focus, however, was not on socializing but on academics and tennis—especially tennis. Morgan was a tough coach who pushed his athletes, and he also brought in some of the tennis world's great players to meet and sometimes play with the students. This was how Arthur got to meet one of his childhood idols, the great Mexican-born player Pancho Gonzalez. Gonzalez recognized Arthur's talents immediately and took an interest in him, becoming a kind of informal coach during his early years at UCLA.

The competition with other tennis players at UCLA was tough. The school had a lot of white players who had been trained at the best whites-only clubs with the best trainers. Arthur worked hard to perfect his game, and in 1961 he was ranked 29th in the men's division of the USLTA. His friend Charlie Pasarell was ranked slightly ahead of him.

During his college years, Arthur came to know many young tennis players who were on their way up in the sport. In addition to Charlie, Arthur befriended Donald Dell, who in later years would become his manager. He also met a number of young men who became opponents on the college tennis circuit. One of these was Dennis Ralston, who was a student at rival USC and a year ahead of Arthur. Dennis and Ralston were paired against each other at numerous matches throughout their college years. In a classic match in 1964, Ashe, representing UCLA, opposed Ralston, representing USC, at the Southern California Intercollegiates. The match was hard fought, and in the end, Arthur won. Their final while they were in college was at the National Intercollegiates, and in this match, Ralston triumphed. Arthur became friends with most of his court opponents, including Ralston. Another opponent who became a very close friend in later life was Stan Smith, who would accompany Arthur to South Africa in 1973. Another opponent and friend was Dave Reed, who faced Arthur in the finals of a college tournament in California toward the end of Arthur's freshman year. Arthur easily defeated Reed in this match, and the next year, they went on to become college roommates.

Now—finally—with an established although still somewhat untested reputation, Arthur began to be invited to play in major regional tournaments. The signs of the times were evident in the United States. The civil rights revolution would soon be in full force, and before long, all the racial barriers Arthur had faced as a young man would be swept away in tennis. In 1962, Arthur played as an adult in his first U.S. National Championship at Forest Hills. He was defeated in the second round, but the point was he had played in this tournament—the pinnacle of U.S. competition—and he would play there again.

In 1963, Arthur played for the first time at that great temple of tennis, Wimbledon. Getting to England, however, proved to be a challenge. Many white tennis players could easily afford the cost of the trip themselves or had sponsors who would pay the costs, which included airplane fare, hotels, and the price of food. But Arthur and his family were not rich. To raise money for the trip, Dr. Johnson, his old coach, asked friends and supporters for donations, and the black high schools of Richmond took up collections. This was a moving tribute that touched Arthur deeply as he realized that so many black kids, who had little money to begin with, were willing to dig into their pockets to help one of their native sons.

With this assistance, Arthur flew to London in the summer of 1963 for his first Wimbledon tournament. At 20 years of age, this was his first trip abroad, and he was thrilled and fascinated to be in England—and to play at the venerable All-England club, with its revered traditions in tennis. Arthur won his first two matches before being defeated in the third round by Chuck McKinley, ranked as the number-one player in the United States, who went on to win the tournament. It was a very distinguished first-time effort at such an important tournament, and Arthur could feel justly proud of his performance. The sights and sounds of England were thrilling to Arthur, not only at Wimbledon but in historic London. He felt a long way from home in Richmond, Virginia.

Back in the United States, Arthur prepared for the 1963 tournament at Forest Hills. Before the tournament, however, he received news that he had always hoped would come: he had been named to the Davis Cup team. The appointment was the beginning of a long and distinguished relationship between Arthur and Davis Cup play.

JOINING THE DAVIS CUP TEAM

The Davis Cup is an international competition in which teams from different countries compete against each other. It took its name from the original 13-inch-high trophy that was named for Dwight F. Davis, an

American who was a Harvard student at the time that he became one of the founders of the competition in 1900. His goal in founding the competition was to stimulate international good will by fostering friendly competition between tennis teams from different countries.

In the 1960s and even today, not every American tennis player wanted to play Davis Cup matches. They were not a good source of income, especially when the purses associated with the big tournaments began to grow after the 1960s. But many players—Arthur Ashe among them—were proud to represent their country in a team capacity and gladly played Davis Cup matches. In later life, Ashe wrote, "Segregation and racism had made me loathe aspects of the white South but had left me scarcely less of a patriot."[1] Playing on the Davis Cup team did not guarantee that a player would necessarily participate in many matches. In fact, between 1963 and 1978, Arthur played Davis Cup tennis, he played a total of only 32 Davis Cup matches, winning 27 of them.[2] After his retirement from tennis, he served (1980–1985) as captain of the U.S. Davis Cup team, which he considered another of the highlights of his life (see chapter 5).

When Bob Kelleher, then the captain of the U.S. Davis Cup team, asked Ashe to join, Arthur was overwhelmed with happiness, but he was not totally surprised. He knew he was a good player. He also realized this was a historic moment. He was the first African American to be on the team; he would go down in history for that fact alone.

FINISHING COLLEGE—AND BEYOND

By the time Arthur began his final two years in college, his standing in the tennis world had risen to new heights. By 1963, he was ranked as the sixth best player in the United States. And with his selection to be on the Davis Cup team, his name became known across the country. In 1964, Arthur played Wimbledon again, but this time, because of his growing fame, the USLTA paid for his travel expenses. Arthur made it to the fourth round before being defeated by one of the world's best players, the Australian Roy Emerson. After Wimbledon, Arthur again played at Forest Hills, this time being defeated in the third round.

In his final full year in college (1964–1965), Arthur's tennis ranking rose to number three in the United States. He was named captain of the UCLA tennis team, and he continued to play college tennis as well as tournaments and exhibitions for charity. Although his full-time college days were almost over, Arthur still needed a few more credits to graduate, but he decided to postpone these courses until the spring of 1966 in order to travel with the Davis Cup team on a tour of Australia, where team members were scheduled to play in a number of tournaments.

Australia was a challenging place to play. Not only was this Arthur's first invitation to travel abroad with the Davis Cup team, it was to a country that was producing some of the greatest tennis players in the world, some of whom, like Rod Laver and Roy Emerson, had already beaten Arthur on the court. On the trip, Arthur won three regional tournaments and got into the finals of the big match, the Australian national championships, where he was beaten again by Roy Emerson. The world of Australian tennis was dazzled by Arthur, who was more and more becoming a media figure. In addition, at the end of 1965, his amateur ranking rose to number two in the country. He now turned his attention to finishing the credits he needed for graduation—and then to fulfilling a responsibility that young men faced in the 1960s.

Long before he finished his studies, Arthur had to make an important decision about his post-college career. In the 1960s, the United States was becoming involved in a war in Southeast Asia, in Vietnam. At the time, young men of 18 faced the draft—being called up to the army for two years of service. Young men had to face the reality of military service—and the possibility that they might be sent overseas to fight in a war in Asia.

There other options to waiting for a draft notice. At UCLA, Arthur was a member of the Reserve Officers Training Corps—the ROTC— a military training program under which a young man would receive a small stipend from the government, to be used toward his education. In return, an ROTC member would be obligated for army service after college but would enter the service as an officer. In either case—as an officer or as an enlisted man—young men in the 1960s faced this serious interruption of their careers. It was an obligation that had to be faced, one way or another. Following the Forest Hills tournament of 1966, Arthur reported for duty in the U.S. Army.

ARMY SERVICE

Arthur did his two months of basic training in Washington State, after which he was commissioned as a second lieutenant in the U.S. Army. At a time when many young men were being sent to Vietnam, where the pace of American involvement was increasing in the mid-1960s, Arthur was lucky in his assignment. He was sent to the U.S. Military Academy at West Point, on the Hudson River in New York. There he would work as a data processor (which made use of his academic background as a business major), and he would also be a tennis coach. It was an ideal assignment, and one that allowed Arthur to maintain his connection with the game of tennis. The program at West Point stressed both academics and sports—all kinds of sports, including tennis. Arthur was the right person to take charge of the West Point tennis program.

Arthur was a patriotic young man. At a time when the war in Vietnam was becoming increasingly unpopular, and when young people were using many different means to avoid military service, Arthur willingly accepted his obligation. He knew he would be criticized by some African Americans for not speaking out against the war, but at this stage in his young life, Arthur was not someone who made bold statements on social issues of the time. That would change as he got older. But between 1966 and 1969, he did his service in the Army.

By the time he left the military, the world of tennis had changed in a dramatic way.

NOTES

1. Ashe, *Days of Grace,* p. 66.
2. Ibid., p. 67.

Chapter 3

THE TOP OF
THE TENNIS WORLD

Until the late 1960s, Arthur Ashe played tennis as an amateur. The tennis world up to that time was divided between amateurs and professionals. All the prestigious tennis tournaments such as Wimbledon and the national championships of the United States, France, and Australia were reserved for amateur players only. The word *amateur* did not mean that a tennis player had fewer skills than a professional player. It meant that amateurs did not play for money to support themselves. Amateur tennis events like Wimbledon were not played for money, but for the prestige of winning the trophy. Professional tennis players, by contrast, played the game to make as much money as they could. There were tournaments for professionals, but they did not have the prestige and renown that the great amateur tournaments did. In addition, professionals made money working, for example, as tennis directors at expensive tennis clubs or luxury hotels or as private coaches. Amateurs, by contrast, were not allowed to accept money for playing tennis of any kind if they wanted to preserve their amateur status.

There were advantages and disadvantages to each status. An amateur player could play the great historic national tournaments and win the titles that would forever mark them as great tennis players. There was nothing greater in the tennis world, for example, than a trophy from Wimbledon. No amount of money could buy that kind of prestige. On the other hand, being a professional meant one could earn unlimited amounts of money and at the same time be doing what one loved best. And at a point in most people's lives, making a living to support one's family becomes all important.

TENNIS COMES OF AGE

By the late 1960s, many in the tennis world realized that this distinction between amateurs and professionals was outmoded and served no good purpose. It was a holdover from an old era when tennis was a "gentleman's" game, when some people thought that playing tennis for money was vulgar and beneath the dignity of the game. The reality in the modern world was that tennis players, like any other athletes, needed to support themselves. Very few, if any, tennis players came from wealthy, aristocratic families, as had been the case in England in the nineteenth century. In Arthur's day, most of the talented players came through the colleges and universities. When a young person graduated from college, he or she needed to make money, the world of amateur tennis prevented talented players from earning a living playing the game.

At the same time, any rising tennis star would not necessarily want to leave the amateur world too quickly, because turning professional would cut off the possibility of playing in the Grand Slam events. Professional tennis players were among the best the world had to offer. Why should they be excluded from competing in the Grand Slam events?

By the late 1960s and 1970s, tennis players were also becoming "stars" in their own right. The coverage of tennis matches on TV created a whole new audience for tennis, which previously had been restricted to people who could afford to buy tickets to attend tennis matches. As tennis gained a wider audience, tennis personalities emerged—and many of these personalities were very different from the type of people who had played tennis in earlier years. Some, like Arthur Ashe, were widely loved and admired for the skill of their game and their manners and dignity on the court. Others, many of whom Arthur would play against and later manage on the Davis Cup team, were self-centered and at times rude. But they were always talented players, and they probably commanded as much attention as they did by their antics on the court as much as by the skill of their game. Most of the outrageous behavior on the court came from male players. A new generation of "bad boys" of tennis became famous, noted not only for their incredible skill at the game but for challenging line calls that went against them, for sometimes cursing on the court, for slamming their rackets to the ground when things did not go their way, or for yelling back at fans in the stands who were perhaps taunting them. They were sometimes hated and sometimes loved—some fans seemed to enjoy the bad behavior—but they were clearly talented and could not be forgotten.

The change that rippled through the tennis world in the late 1960s was initiated—as modern tennis had been—by the All-England club at

Wimbledon. In late 1967, the English club announced that the Wimbledon tournament would henceforth be an "open" tournament—both amateurs and professionals would be allowed to compete. A few months later, the International Lawn Tennis Association (ILTA) voted in favor of open tennis. In 1968, while still in the army, Arthur played in the first open tournament at Wimbledon. He played exceedingly good tennis but was defeated by Rod Laver in the semifinals.

Arthur's schedule for the next few months was crowded. There were the Davis Cup matches against Spain in Cleveland, Ohio (won by the U.S. team), followed by the U.S. amateur national championships a few days later in Massachusetts, which Arthur won against an old friend, Bob Lutz. A week later, the first U.S. Open would be held at Forest Hills. (In 1968, the USLTA decided to hold one final amateur tournament before going over completely to open tennis.)

WINNING THE U.S. OPEN

It had been 11 years since Althea Gibson—an African American female and one of Dr. Johnson's top tennis students in Richmond—had won at Wimbledon and at the U.S. national championships at Forest Hills. It was 1968, four years after the passage of the 1964 Civil Rights Act, and still some racial barriers could be found in the world of whites-only tennis clubs. No African American man had duplicated the feats of Althea Gibson. In the fall of 1968, Arthur Ashe was poised to become the first African American male to rise to the win a Grand Slam title.

But his victory at the first U.S. Open seemed a long shot. The field was crowded with all the best male players from around the world, including Rod Laver, as well as many members of the U.S. Davis Cup team. Arthur did not believe he would be able to get past Laver. But then, in one of those moments of luck that one has no control over, Laver was defeated unexpectedly by another player early in the tournament. From that point on, Arthur progressed steadily to the finals.

In the final match, he faced Tom Okker, a talented player from the Netherlands. The game was brutal, going to a full five sets in back-and-forth play that had both players on top at various points in the match. Finally, in the fifth set, Arthur prevailed. He had won the first U.S. Open. In the stands were his father and Dr. Johnson, who had come up from Richmond for the occasion. After the match, the television commentator Bud Collins was heading back to the press box when he came upon Arthur's father standing alone in a passageway underneath the stadium. He was weeping. Collins asked him if anything was all right, and Arthur Sr. replied, "Oh God, yes, everything is wonderful. But when I think of that boy ... and to come to this day."[1] It had been an inspiring journey for an unknown young black boy from a poor family in the South who just happened to like to swing a tennis racket on the courts of Brook Field in Richmond.

The beginning of the open era did not bring Arthur a lot of money, at least at first. He was still an amateur, so he was not eligible for the $100,000 prize that was offered to the winner of the U.S. Open. The only way he could have claimed that prize was to become a professional, which, of course, he could not do until after his army service was completed. Before his discharge, Arthur journeyed to Australia to play in the Davis Cup finals against that country. The United States won, which meant that Arthur's name would be etched for all time on the Davis Cup trophy. By the end of 1968, he also received the highest ranking tennis could offer: Arthur Ashe was ranked as the number-one player in the world. (Official rankings are calculated by a complex formula that takes into consideration the number of one's victories and the specific tournaments that were won.) Arthur would never win the U.S. Open again, although until his retirement he competed every year except 1977 and 1979. In 1972 he reached the finals again, but he was beaten by the flamboyant Romanian player Ilie Nastase. Nevertheless, the U.S. Open would always hold a special place in his heart, and in the years after his retirement, he always made an effort to attend U.S. Open matches.

Arthur had decided that after his army service, he would turn professional. Now there was no reason not to. Under the new open system, he could participate in all the prestigious Grand Slam events as a professional, and he could also start to earn a living. Arthur's father had always worked hard and supported his family, but the Ashes were not rich, and Arthur's early years in tennis had been a financial strain. He believed it was time for him to use his talent to make money and bring security not only to himself but to his father. Arthur realized his father had sacrificed for his tennis career, and he wanted to give back.

Arthur was released from military service in February 1969. At the age of 25, he had many good years of tennis ahead of him. By turning pro, his schedule became much fuller, with entry now into the professional tournaments and with many commercial opportunities to consider. Because he was one of the top players in the world, many companies wanted to pay Arthur to endorse their products, to be their spokesman. Arthur accepted invitations to endorse a brand of tennis racket as well as a line of tennis clothing. He also became the tennis professional at the exclusive Doral Country Club in Miami, Florida, and conducted tennis seminars for corporations. The Doral job was a pleasant job to have. He was responsible for the tennis program that the country club offered its guests: tennis lessons, charity and exhibition matches, and the like. In addition, he was provided a suite of rooms at the hotel where he could stay whenever he was in Miami. As he later wrote, "I long ago decided that, on the whole, I much prefer having money to not having it. In that sense, it makes me happy."[2]

Arthur came too early into the open era to earn the millions and millions of dollars that top players earn today, but he earned considerable amounts, and he invested what he earned wisely. His involvement in tennis included being a founding member, in 1972, of the Association of Tennis Professionals (ATP), a player's union established to stand up for the rights and needs of players. In 1973, for example, the ILTA barred a Yugoslavian player from competing in the Wimbledon tournament because he had refused to play a Davis Cup match. Arthur and other members of the ATP believed this was an unjust ruling and boycotted Wimbledon that year. The ILTA, he believed, was a reactionary organization, and it and the leaders of the four Grand Slam events needed to be counterbalanced by an organization that served as a voice for the players. Not all the top players joined the ATP—some were very conservative and did not believe in any collective action on the part of players, while others wanted to fend for themselves and not be considered part of a group—but Arthur, as a founder of the organization, remained active in it and served a term (1974–1975) as its president.

WINNING THE AUSTRALIAN OPEN

In Arthur's first years as a professional, his game remained at a high level. If he was not ranked number one, he was always in the top five. In 1970, Arthur won another Grand Slam title: the Australian Open. Australians love tennis, and their Open was always held in January, which is the height of summertime in Australia. The Open was held in the Kooyong district of Melbourne, on grass courts. In the 1980s, the Australian Open was moved to Melbourne Park, next to the Melbourne Cricket Club, in a new arena named for the great Australian player Rod Laver. With this move, the Australian Open became a tournament played on hard courts, not grass. (Tennis players are usually stronger on one type of court over another, depending on how they grew up playing the game. Most Americans are trained on hard courts, where the ball has a higher and quicker bounce. When they play on grass courts, such as Wimbledon, they are forced to adapt their game to the slightly different back-and-forth that results from a grass surface.)

Arthur won the Australian Open against R. D. Cleary in straight sets. It was a great triumph and came just 16 months after his win in the U.S. Open. Arthur had always enjoyed playing in Australia. The Australians were exuberant fans who rooted heartily for their countrymen but always appreciated the talents of the opposing players. In addition, they were fond of Americans and liked Arthur Ashe as a man and a champion. Winning his first competition in their Open was a special honor. The following year, 1971, he got as far as the finals but was defeated. He played again in the Australian Open only in 1977 and 1978 but never progressed passed the semifinals. Still, he had two Grand Slam tournaments to his credit by the time he had turned 27.

WINNING WIMBLEDON

There was one tennis trophy, however, that all players crave: Wimbledon. But by the mid-1970s, it seemed that this title was beyond Arthur's grasp. He was now in his early 30s, which is not young for a tennis player, and he had not won a Grand Slam title since his win in the singles tournament in the Australian Open. In addition, many younger players, who were strong and fast, were now coming up and dominating the game. Still, Arthur hoped and would not give up the possibility that he would one day win the coveted Wimbledon trophy.

In 1975, Arthur was about to turn 32, and he was playing very good tennis. In the months leading up to Wimbledon, he won a number of professional tournaments, such as his victory in Dallas in May of that year, and he was in good shape for the All-England competition. Still, the competition looked formidable. Many observers believed he would never get past the quarterfinals, in which he faced the nineteen-year-old Swedish star Bjorn Borg. Borg was already one of the greatest tennis players the game had ever known, and everyone thought he would crush Arthur. But Arthur surprised them all by winning. It was not supposed to happen, but it did. The older American beat the young Swede. Arthur went onto the semifinals, in which he defeated Tony Roche, an Australian player.

Then came the final match—and it proved to be one of the most anticipated and exciting pairings in Wimbledon history. Facing Arthur was the number-one American male tennis player at the moment, Jimmy Connors. Young and brash, Connors was in many ways the exact opposite of Arthur on the court. When calls did not go his way, he would often lose his temper, shake his head in disgust, or talk loudly to himself. He could be rude and self-centered—and he was one of the greatest tennis players of all time. What distinguished Connors at this point in his career was his swiftness on the court. There was seemingly no shot, however far down the line, that was beyond his reach. That plus the accuracy of his returns made him hard to beat.

Long before the 1975 Wimbledon finals, Arthur and Jimmy Connors had a troubled relationship. On the surface, they seemed to have more in common than not. Connors was white, but, like Arthur, he came from a family that did not have much money. Also like Arthur, he had a single parent who had greatly influenced the course his life took. Connors's career had been guided by his formidable mother, who had led her son from the modest blue-collar neighborhood of his birth and managed his career all the way to the pinnacle of the tennis world.

But the similarities ended there. Arthur was supremely devoted to Davis Cup tennis. Connors refused to play Davis Cup. Ashe was a founder of and a believer in the ATP. Connors refused to join the players' union. But these differences were minor compared to the bad feelings that erupted when Arthur seemed to question Connors's patriotism for refusing to play Davis Cup tennis. Arthur had chosen his words carefully saying that Connors was "seemingly unpatriotic" in refusing to play for his country.[3] Connors was furious at the remark and filed a multimillion-dollar lawsuit for libel against Ashe. Arthur probably should not have said these words, but he did, and it was an indication of how strongly he felt about Davis Cup play and also, perhaps, about the younger generation's attitudes and behavior toward tennis—especially their responsibilities as famous athletes.

With this background of ill will between them, the two strode onto the center court at Wimbledon on June 23, 1975, before an audience of hundreds of expectant Americans, British royalty, European tennis fans, and family and friends. Before the match, Arthur and a group of friends had discussed the best strategy for defeating Connors. They were well aware that Connors played a strong and agile game. He was young, quick, and could be all over the court in seconds. The best tactic, Arthur realized, was to hit balls directly at Connors and to force him to make backhand returns. Connor's backhand shots were not his strongest. When balls came at him indirectly, Connors could hit deadly accurate angle shots that exhausted his opponent by forcing him to race and back and forth over the court. Tom Okker, whom Arthur had defeated for the U.S. Open title in 1968, was in the audience that day at Wimbledon. He had experienced Arthur as a power player, someone who hit hard shots and was able to serve lots of aces. Okker noticed that on this occasion,

Arthur was hitting softer shots from time to time. He was varying his game to meet the special challenge that Connors presented.[4]

The strategy worked. Hitting balls directly at Connors, and getting close to the net as quickly as possible, Ashe overwhelmed Connors in the first two sets. Connors seemed confused by Arthur's tactics and could not find an adequate response. Connors rallied in the third set, but Arthur came back in the fourth and won the match 6-1, 6-1, 5-7, 6-4. At the age of 32, he finally held the Wimbledon trophy over his head. The victory was all the more sweet because it was not expected. Arthur had played an exceedingly intelligent game, and, as always, kept his cool under pressure. In addition, the audience was clearly rooting for Arthur and did not like Connors, who at that point in his young life could not shake the reputation for being an unpleasant presence on the court—a character trait particularly disliked by the tradition-loving British audiences. There was one regret for Arthur: unfortunately, Dr. Johnson was no longer alive to see his student win the coveted Wimbledon title. For Arthur Sr. it was another unbelievable moment. He had traveled to England from Richmond to witness his son's triumph. It was as emotional a moment as Arthur's U.S. Open victory in 1968.

For Connors, his loss of Wimbledon in 1975 was a devastating defeat. He would go on to great victories, including Wimbledon, in a career that spanned another 20 years. And, as he got older, the negative, troublesome image that plagued him as a youth would fade, and he would become a greatly loved player admired for his enormous talent and courage on the court. After the Wimbledon loss in 1975, Connors quietly dropped his lawsuit against Arthur.

The Wimbledon title was Arthur's third—and, as it would turn out, final—Grand Slam title. His active career as a tennis player was winding down. But he would remain active in the game in the years immediately after he stopped playing—in Davis Cup play, which he had loved as a player and would soon lead as the captain of the team.

NOTES

1. Towle, Mike, *I Remember Arthur Ashe: Memories of a True Tennis Pioneer and Champion of Social Causes by the People Who Knew Him* (Nashville, TN: Cumberland House, 2001), p. 16.

2. Ashe, *Days of Grace*, p. 196.

3. Ibid., p. 79.

4. Towle, *I Remember Arthur Ashe*, pp. 26–27.

Chapter 4

OPPORTUNITIES AND CHALLENGES

The Wimbledon victory in 1975 thrust Arthur into a world of new opportunity and responsibility. His life was no longer simply about playing tennis. Now he could socialize easily with the elite from the highest levels of society, all over the world. His image appeared on the cover of magazines; articles were written about him, and he was interviewed on TV. More and more people knew who he was. He had become, in modern terminology, a media star. And he continued to make more money than he had ever made in his life.

As a person who was almost constantly in the news, Arthur became increasingly aware of other kinds of responsibilities he now had the freedom to exercise. As a young man, he had not been outspoken in the emerging civil rights movement, even though he had felt the sting of discrimination and segregation from the time he was a child. His father and Dr. Johnson had something to do with the development of his cautious approach to life's challenges. Both men were not the type who engaged in social protest or vocal demonstrations against injustice. This did not mean that they were afraid to speak out. But both Arthur Sr. and Dr. Johnson believed that change could come about if one worked quietly from the inside, day by day, step by step.

The lessons Arthur learned from his father and Dr. Johnson were important when he was a young player. He never would have been allowed to advance as far as he did had he had the personality of a Jimmy Connors. The white tennis world may have winced at the bad behavior of a Connors, but it tolerated it. It is doubtful that an African American player would have been allowed to act in the same way, simply because of the prejudice that existed at the time. A white boy could get away with behavior that would have resulted in a black boy being kicked out of the game.

But by the late 1970s, the world had changed and so had Arthur. He was no longer an unknown kid from Richmond trying to break into a sport dominated by white people. He was at the top of that sport—and, he realized, he could afford to take risks and do things in different ways, in ways that might perhaps even surprise people who had a notion of him as a polite young man who never complained about anything. An early expression of his determination had been his role as a founder of the players' union, the Association of Tennis Professionals (ATP), which in itself was a step in the direction of a kind of activism he would pursue later in life.

FIGHTING APARTHEID

But Arthur had never ever forgotten who he was and where he came from. As one of the top players of the world, and as a deeply respected young American, he could now face issues of race. He had a platform and a voice that was recognized around the world. In 1969, 1970, and 1971, Arthur was denied a visa to play in the South African Open competition. South Africa, a huge country at the southern tip of the continent of Africa, was ruled by its white minority. The majority of South Africans were black, but they had no rights at all. They could not vote, they were barred from certain professions, and they could not live in certain areas of the country. Their separation from the white population was rigidly enforced by a legal system called apartheid, an Afrikaans word meaning "apart" or "separated" from. (Afrikaans is the language of white South Africans who were the descendants of the original Dutch colonists. The Dutch were the first European to settle in the region.) Apartheid also applied to what the white government in South Africa categorized as "colored" people—this included people, for example, of South Asian origin. There were many settlers in South Africa whose ancestors came from India, and these people were categorized as "colored." "Colored" meant you were not quite as low on the totem pole as native blacks, but you were still not white enough to enjoy full civil rights and liberties. "Colored" people were not excluded as rigidly from all aspects of daily life as were black people, but they had no political rights.

How did such a terrible system of government come about? The first Europeans to settle in South Africa arrived in the year 1652. They were Dutch, and they worked for the Dutch East India Company. Their settlement was near what is now the large city of Cape Town, at the extreme tip of South Africa. The Dutch began to move inland, and as they did so, they came into contact with native peoples, and conflict soon erupted. In the early 1800s, English settlers also began to arrive in South Africa, adding to the volatile mix of peoples. The Dutch (who came to be called "Boers") also quarreled with the English. When diamonds and gold were discovered in South Africa in the late 1800s, the conflicts became more intense as the Dutch and English fought for control of this rich land.

The Dutch eventually prevailed after a war with the British in the 1890s, sometimes called the Boer War, but they were never sure how they should govern the native peoples, who vastly outnumbered them. In 1948, they invented the system of apartheid. As part of this system designed to separate the races, they created 10 "homelands," which were called "bantustans," where the native black population was to be moved. The white government said these native homelands would one day be independent and governed by black people. In fact, the bantustan territories were scattered over the country and consisted of the poorest lands. The populations were, in actuality, assigned to live in large concentration camps. Most of them had to leave the homeland territories in order to work in the white areas of South Africa. When they did so, they had to carry identity cards, were subjected to curfews, and were victimized by all the harsh laws of apartheid.

Apartheid oppressed millions of people and kept them in abject poverty. Arthur Ashe, one of the greatest tennis players in the world, was excluded from the South African Open for one reason: he was black. It did not matter that he was an American: he was black. And this exclusion insulted and irritated him. He decided to do something about it. In the late 1960s, the attention of the world had not yet been directed at the issue of apartheid. Other concerns—such as the Cold War between the United States and the Soviet Union—had worldwide implications and seemed more important than the racial policies, however unjust, of a country at the extreme tip of southern Africa. Arthur Ashe played a role in helping direct the spotlight on apartheid. In 1969 he appeared before a committee of the United Nations and urged that organization to take action against South Africa. He spoke out against apartheid and was successful in getting South Africa expelled from Davis Cup play. South Africa had, in fact, won the Davis Cup in 1974 by default. The finals were between South Africa and India, but the Indian team, as a way of protesting apartheid refused to play South Africa, and, as a result, the Davis Cup was awarded to South Africa. After this embarrassment, Davis Cup officials decided to bar South Africa from competition because of the nation's apartheid policy. For the conservative world of tennis, this action represented a big step in the fight against racism.

But the South African tennis community, run by whites, continued to sponsor an Open tournament, and Arthur continued to apply. With each rejection, the South African government came under more and more international scrutiny.

JOURNEY TO SOUTH AFRICA

Finally, in 1973, the South African government granted Arthur a visa that would allow him to enter the country and play in the South African Open. In London, just before his flight to Johannesburg, Arthur met with a delegation of South Africans who pleaded with him not to make the trip. They believed that a black man—and an American—who traveled to South Africa to play in their whites-only national tennis tournament would be granting legitimacy to the apartheid government, simply by appearing in the country. Arthur listened to them politely but disagreed. As he later wrote, he remained convinced "that my way is the one that can best serve the purpose of eventual equality."[1]

So he flew to South Africa. The arrival terminal at the Johannesburg airport was a surprise to Arthur. There was no sign of apartheid policies that were in force throughout the country—the terminal, which was the first impression of the country that foreigners received—was carefully designed to show almost no signs of apartheid. Nor did Arthur encounter the most brutal signs of apartheid in his first hours in the country once he had left the airport. Instead of staying in a hotel, Arthur had been invited to stay at the home of a wealthy Jewish South African real estate developer named Brian Young. A dinner party was given at Young's home that first night, and a black household servant came up to Arthur to take his drink order. After he had ordered his drink, the woman said "Yes, master." Arthur was upset by the woman's response. He was a poor black kid from the American South who had experienced discrimination while growing up, and it made him uncomfortable to have another black person call him "master." This was a small moment, but it was an unmistakable introduction to the class system that divided South African society—and this in the home of a white man, Brian Young, who was opposed to apartheid![2]

When Arthur went to the tennis courts the next day, he saw his first "Whites Only" sign, in English and also in Afrikaans (in glaring capital letters, "HERE BLANKES"—for "white men only", and "DAMAS BLANKES"—for "white women only"). Blacks and whites were required to sit in different sections of the court, had different bathrooms, different drinking fountains, and even different entrances and exits. The signs reminded Arthur that South Africa was really a police state, and that there was no freedom at all—for anyone. Arthur had the chance to meet a number of black South African tennis players. He noticed immediately that they were not very skilled players, unlike the many white South Africans he had met over the years, who were all very good competitors. This did not surprise him. Black South African tennis players had poor facilities, little training, and no star players from their own people who could train them and serve as mentors. Arthur was deeply saddened by this reality.

But the true devastation and cruelty of apartheid struck Arthur when he visited the vast black ghetto of Soweto, 17 miles from Johannesburg, on November 20, 1973. Bowing to international pressure, the South African government had reluctantly allowed Arthur into the country. But it had imposed the condition that he not make political statements during his visit. A trip to the notorious Soweto might be considered a political statement in itself, even if Arthur made no public comment. The South Africa government did not want a prominent American whom everyone knew was opposed to apartheid to be roaming around the streets of what was perhaps the most notorious symbol of apartheid, Soweto. But Arthur had come this far, and there was no way he was not going to visit Soweto, where more than a million black South Africans lived in terrible, hopeless poverty.

From the time of his arrival in South Africa, Arthur assumed he was being tailed by the South African police, and his journey to Soweto confirmed that he was being watched. He was not surprised or particularly upset. With the police tracking him so closely, he knew it was less likely that something bad would happen to him in public at the hands of an angry white man. Soweto, short for Southwestern Township, was more of a gigantic reservation whose inhabitants were forced to live in its squalid shacks and to walk miles to the nearest railroad station to travel into Johannesburg to their low-paying jobs. Arthur was horrified, angered, and saddened by what he saw. The people were very friendly to him, and most seemed happy to see him, but the experience was depressing nonetheless. He returned to Johannesburg, more determined than ever to fight this inhuman injustice.

Arthur believed that he, like the South African government, had certain conditions that needed to be met if he were to play in South Africa. He insisted that during his matches there be no segregated seating in the stadium. When he played his first match at the segregated Ellis Park, some of the officials were upset and confused when they saw blacks and "coloreds" sitting in previously whites-only seats. Arthur won his first match before this integrated audience. The match was held in the middle of the week, and the attendance was not that high because people were working. Nevertheless, it was a historic game.

Some later matches were segregated, and Arthur realized he had been naïve to expect that the oppressive government of South Africa would bow to his wishes. An interesting match in the tournament was between Arthur and the white South African Cliff Drysdale. Drysdale was an outspoken opponent of apartheid, and Arthur sensed that in an odd way, a large part of the white audience was rooting for him over Drysdale, whom they considered a traitor to their race. Arthur won the hard-fought match. The next day he returned to Soweto to give a tennis clinic for young people. This time, he stayed longer than his first visit a couple of days before. After the clinic, he was surrounded by a crowd of Soweto citizens, this time somewhat less friendly than on his first visit. Some of them called out and told him to "go home." Others, however, were thrilled to see this black man, this American who had achieved so much in his life. He was, for them, a man who gave them hope.

Arthur made it as far as the finals in the South African tournament, where he was defeated by Jimmy Connors, whom he would defeat two years later for the Wimbledon crown. Arthur was disappointed by the loss. He would have loved to see the South African tennis crown go to a black man, but it was not to be. Connors was young and one of the best players in the world. In this match, he was simply better than Arthur, and he won it fair and square. Before the tournament was over, Arthur played doubles tennis with Tom Okker, his opponent in the 1968 U.S. Open, and they won the doubles final. Although he had lost the singles crown, the victory in the doubles was something he could be proud of. In addition, he won the title jointly with a white man. It was a sharp lesson to the white establishment in South Africa that a white person and a black person could work together harmoniously and, in this case, win a strongly contested competition.

Everywhere he went Arthur created a sensation. Stan Smith, who at the time was ranked as the number-one player in world, was astonished at the reception Arthur received. He said, "Arthur, I mean, you're like God here, and they don't even recognize that I'm here." Another friend pointed out to Smith that Arthur's popularity was easy to understand— the majority of the people in South Africa were black, and Arthur was a hero to them.[3] At one point, Arthur noticed a young black teenage boy following him around near the stadium. Arthur asked what he was doing, and the young boy said that Arthur was the first free black man he had ever seen. Arthur was deeply moved by this moment and vowed to continue his fight against apartheid.[4]

Arthur's decision to go to South Africa continued to be controversial. In the United States, while speaking at Howard University, a black school in Washington, D.C., Arthur was heckled by some students who called him an "Uncle Tom," an insulting term derived from Harriet Beecher Stowe's novel *Uncle Tom's Cabin* (1851–1852) An Uncle Tom refers to a black person who is subservient and ingratiating to whites and cooperates with his or her oppressor. Arthur was shocked to be treated with such open disrespect. He realized, as he continued to speak, that the students doing the heckling were South African blacks, and he decided to confront them. He asked why they were hiding at comfortable schools in the United States instead of fighting against apartheid in their country. They did not respond, and he was allowed to finish his talk without further interruption.

Arthur made no apologies for his position and tactics in fighting apartheid. He had been instrumental in getting South Africa barred from Davis Cup play, and he spoke out forcefully against the system. His decision to go to South Africa was motivated as much by a desire to see the situation up close and in person as it was by any desire to win another tennis title—especially that one. The trip had reinforced his determination to speak out against apartheid and to fight oppression throughout the world. Arthur's activism against apartheid would continue into the last years of his life and would become more open as he took more risks in expressing his opposition to this oppression.

BROADENING HORIZONS

Arthur's horizons were expanding in other ways during the 1970s. His relationships with corporations brought not only income but the ability to travel the country and promote tennis. He now had an apartment in Manhattan, in New York City, and he spent a lot of time at the Doral Club in Miami. He also made himself available as a goodwill ambassador for the U.S. State Department, traveling the world representing his country and promoting its image in the tennis world. In addition to his concerns about South Africa, Arthur took an interest in other African affairs in general, as well. He became involved in TransAfrica, an organization established by black members of the U.S. Congress and chaired by a childhood friend from Richmond, Randall Robinson. TransAfrica was a think tank, a research organization that studied issues relating to Africa and lobbied for legislation that would benefit Africa in any way. It was the only think tank in the United States controlled exclusively by African Americans.

In addition, Arthur was a founder of Artists and Athletes Against Apartheid, which he cochaired with the black actor Harry Belafonte. One of its goals was to try to persuade artists and athletes not to perform in South Africa. Arthur was well aware that he had played in South Africa, but as soon as the United Nations had voted to impose economic sanctions against South Africa, Arthur believed it was important that they be enforced, meaning that entertainers and athletes stay out of the country until apartheid was abolished.

Arthur often wondered if his activism against apartheid was an effort on his part to make up for the years he had not been strongly involved in the American civil rights movement. He later wrote, "While blood was running freely in the streets of Birmingham, Memphis, and Biloxi, I had been playing tennis," a fact that caused him later to feel, in his own words, "a burning sense of shame."[5] The assassination of the great civil rights leader Dr. Martin Luther King Jr. in 1968 was a kind of turning point for Arthur. After that searing event, he gradually began to speak out on social issues that affected blacks. At the same, he recognized that he would always be his father's son. He could not undo the training he had had as a boy and man, both on the tennis court and off. He would always be Arthur Ashe, and though he could stand openly for principles of morality and right, he would do it in his way—with politeness, grace, and a sense of respect for all people, even those he disagreed with.

In the late 1970s, Arthur thought briefly of running for the U.S. House of Representatives from his district in Manhattan. The incumbent congressman was a moderate Republican who was popular but not, in Arthur's opinion, unbeatable. After giving the matter some thought, he decided not to go into electoral politics. To run for elective office required a full commitment of time and money, that is, fund-raising. Arthur realized that he did not have the burning desire to be elected to public office. He preferred, instead, to work with such groups as TransAfrica to effect change from the private world. He would continue to represent his country if asked, but, he believed, he could best influence the causes he believed in through the worlds of sports and business.

JEANNE

By the mid 1970s, Arthur Ashe was in his mid-30s. Tennis had given him a wonderful and fulfilled life: championships, popularity, money, and opportunity to speak out on social issues and contribute toward improving the lot of the less fortunate throughout the world. But he lived alone. He had dated from time to time, and, as an attractive and famous young athlete, he never found it difficult to find someone to go out with. But throughout his 20s and 30s, tennis had consumed his life, and he was just ready for marriage.

By the late 1970s, Arthur's years as an active player were coming to an end. Although he had no fixed plans to marry, fate intervened and changed his life. On October 16, 1976, while attending a benefit dinner for the United Negro College Fund at Madison Square Garden in New York City, Arthur could not help but notice an attractive photographer who was taking pictures of all the dignitaries at the event. Her name was Jeanne Moutoussamy, and she was 25 years old and strikingly beautiful. A native of Chicago, she was the daughter of a well-known architect and had two older brothers. Jeanne was a graduate of New York's Cooper Union, where she received a degree in photography. When she met Arthur, she was employed as a graphic artist at the television station WNBC in New York and was also earning income as a freelance photographer.[6]

Arthur was immediately attracted to Jeanne and went out of his way to speak with her. Jeanne later said that Arthur's first approach to her was amusingly clumsy, with him making a remark about how attractive female photographers had become. Still, despite the somewhat goofy introduction, he was Arthur Ashe—handsome, famous, and unattached. Three days later, they went out on their first date. Arthur picked Jeanne up at her office at NBC. Jeanne wanted Arthur to see "who she was" and where she worked.[7] Where she worked, in fact, was a busy office in which she occupied a tiny cubicle, because she was at the beginning of her career.

They fell in love quickly; it did not take them long to discover that they had a lot in common, that they saw the world in the same way, and that they really enjoyed each other's company. When they agreed that they wanted to spend their lives together, it became time to tell their families, and to meet the parents. When Arthur introduced Jeanne to his father, Arthur Sr. remarked how much Jeanne looked like Arthur's late mother. Of mixed African American and East Indian ancestry, Jeanne had long brown hair and a light complexion—as did Arthur's mother. Was this resemblance the initial source of Arthur's attraction? He wondered about it himself, but who can say for sure? One thing was certain: Jeanne was a strong, independent woman, and this quality was one that Arthur found most admirable. Jeanne later said, "I was very independent.... I think those were the things [her independent characteristics] that he loved about me."[8]

Their courtship did not last long. On February 20, 1977, a scant four months after they met, they were married. Jeanne did not want to be called "Mrs. Arthur Ashe." She felt she was a young woman of independent means, with a career of her own, and did not need to submerge her identity by being called Mrs. Ashe. In later years, she decided to be called Jeanne Moutoussamy-Ashe. She realized how proud she was of her husband, and wanted to honor him by taking on his name while at the same time preserving her own.

The wedding ceremony was performed in New York by the Rev. Andrew Young, a friend of Arthur's and a noted veteran of the civil rights movement. In 1977, Young was serving as the U.S. ambassador to the United Nations, a position he had been appointed to by President Jimmy Carter. Arthur was married standing on crutches. He had just had minor surgery 10 days before to remove bone chips from his left heel—a common injury among tennis players. Several years later, Arthur wrote that these crutches were like an omen of the illnesses that would soon plague their young lives.[9]

HEART ATTACK

It was almost an unbelievable illness to strike Arthur Ashe. How could a young man, an athlete in the best possible physical condition, fall victim to heart disease? And at the young age of 36. Wasn't heart disease supposed to be an illness of the old and out-of-shape? The answer to this last question is no. Heart disease can strike at any age, and one of its most important predictors is family history. Unfortunately for Arthur, his immediate family had a history of serious heart disease. His mother had died in her 20s, and one underlying factor in her death was heart disease. Arthur's father had also had a number of minor heart attacks.

Still, no one expected that Arthur, who was in excellent shape, would face a heart problem while still in his 30s. In 1978 and 1979, his game had its ups and downs. At one point, his world ranking had slipped to 257 after his heel surgery. But he fought back, and in 1978 he played Davis Cup tennis and helped the United States regain the trophy. By 1979, his ranking was number five—not a bad place for someone in his mid-30s to be. He was no longer as fast or agile as the younger generation of male tennis players, but he was still formidable on the court. It had been only four years since he defeated one of the fastest players on the court, Jimmy Connors, at Wimbledon. During 1979, he trained hard and completed in a number of professional tournaments. He also continued a full schedule of his good works for charity. It was at one of these events—a tennis clinic for the East River Tennis Club on Long Island on July 31, 1979—that Arthur suffered a heart attack.

The symptoms were unmistakable—severe chest pain, nausea, breath-lessness. Doctors discovered that the main arteries to Arthur's heart, which carried the blood necessary for the heart, were severely blocked. A blockage can cause damage to the heart muscle and can sometimes be fatal. Arthur at first resisted the treatment recommended by his doctors, a bypass operation. This surgery involves adding arteries taken from another part of the body—the leg, for example—and implanting them in the chest cavity, where they can then "bypass" the clogged arteries and carry the vital blood supply necessary for the heart. Arthur did not want to undergo such a drastic operation. In addition, his doctors told him that it was highly unlikely that he would ever play professional tennis again. Although he knew his tennis career was nearing its end, he did not want it to end this way.

Eventually, however, Arthur realized that if he wanted to live, he would have to undergo a quadruple bypass operation, meaning that four major arteries to his heart had to be bypassed with arteries taken from other parts of his body. On December 13, 1979, Arthur had the surgery. It is a lengthy operation that requires the surgeons to crack the bone in the patient's chest that protects the heart, and then take arteries taken from the leg and add them to the heart. Despite the severity of the procedure, Arthur recovered quickly. He was young and in good shape, and aside from the arteries in his heart, the rest of his body was in superb shape. Arthur hoped that he would soon be able to return to the tennis court. But the doctors had been right. Even after the initial stages of his recovery, extreme exertion would lead to chest pain. There was no doubting now that he had to retire from playing tennis.

It was a tough decision, but Arthur made it with the usual grace and dignity that was characteristic of everything he did in life. The announcement to the world was made in April 1980,[10] some four months after his operation. Active tennis play was now in the past. But some of the greatest challenges and successes lay in the future.

NOTES

1. Ashe, Arthur, with Frank Deford, *Arthur Ashe—Portrait in Motion: A Diary* (New York: Carroll & Graf, 1975), p. 114.

2. Ibid., p. 117.

3. Towle, p. 129.

4. Ashe, *Days of Grace*, pp. 112–114.

5. Ibid., pp. 124–125.

6. Ibid., pp. 55–57.

7. Randolph, Laura B., "Jeanne Moutoussamy-Ashe: On Love, Loss, and Life after Arthur," *Ebony*, October 1993.

8. Ibid.

9. Ashe, *Days of Grace*, p. 56.

10. For the text of Arthur's retirement announcement, see the *New York Times*, April 17, 1980.

Chapter 5

DAVIS CUP CAPTAIN

Arthur Ashe had played his last Davis Cup match in 1978. His heart operation and his retirement from active tennis play in 1980, however, did not diminish his love for the Davis Cup tradition. Just a few months after his surgery, Arthur was offered the opportunity of a lifetime. While attending the U.S. Open in New York, he was approached by Marvin P. Richmond, the incoming president of the U.S. Tennis Association (USTA; formerly the USLTA). Richmond told Arthur that Tony Trabert, a former tennis champion and current captain of the U.S. Davis Cup team, wanted to resign. Richmond wanted Ashe to replace Trabert. Trabert, one of the great tennis champions a generation older than Arthur, had been captain of the team since 1976 and had presided over victories against Great Britain in 1978 (in which Arthur had played) and Italy in 1979.

Arthur was ecstatic. This was a dream come true. The captaincy of his beloved Davis Cup team was exactly what he had hoped he could have. Now that he had been sidelined from active play, the Davis Cup team would be an excellent way to keep his hand in the game and to manage a team that represented his country in international play. Little did Arthur know that the adventure he was about to embark on would be, in his own words, "a disorganized, sometimes exhilarating, sometimes frustrating and even humiliating epic of victories and defeats, excitement and tedium, camaraderie and isolation."[1]

DAVIS CUP PLAY

Davis Cup competition is governed by a set of rules established in the early 1900s, when the international tournament was created. Teams from different countries compete against each other as teams. Each round of play consists of five matches between two countries. The first two matches are singles play, and the third is a doubles match. In the final two matches, which are singles games, the contestants from the first two matches play again, but they swap opponents from the first two matches. Contestants may play in singles, doubles, or both—it is up to the captain to decide how best to use the talents of his team.[2] Davis Cup play is a tournament for male players. The women's equivalent is known as the Fed Cup (before 1995, it was called the Federation Cup).

In the United States, Davis Cup play is purely voluntary. Until the early 1980s, a player made no money playing Davis Cup tennis. Expenses were paid (airfare, hotels, and so on), but there was no big prize for the victors. In Arthur's day, one played as a gesture to one's country, for the honor of representing your country in an international competition, in the same way that an athlete participates in the Olympics—not just to win medals, but to represent your country by playing the best you can. The Davis Cup was also a prestigious tradition, and to have been invited to play on the team was a distinct honor.

In the early 1980s, just as Arthur took over as captain of the team, the Davis Cup leadership decided to award prize money. In 1981, a Japanese company put up $1 million to sponsor the competition. In 1983 the NEC Corporation announced that it would donate $2.5 million to the Davis Cup. The winning team would be awarded $200,000 plus a share of the gate receipts. It was a sensible move on the part of the Davis Cup and a recognition that, in the modern world, tennis players competed to earn money. Although these amounts were less than a top player could make playing in Grand Slam and other tournaments (many of which were sponsored by corporations and had big prize money), it was at least something. A player could no longer complain that he could not afford to play the Davis Cup.

The United States had won the first Davis Cup competition, against Great Britain, in 1900. Between 1900 and 1979, the United States won a total of 26 times (1900, 1902, 1913, 1920–1926, 1937–1938, 1946–1949, 1954, 1958, 1963, 1968–1972, and 1978–1979). Play was suspended during World War I (there were no tournaments from 1915 through 1918) and again in World War II (tournaments suspended from 1940 through 1945). Wartime conditions prevented players from traveling, and many were also in the military service of their countries. In addition, many of the competing countries were on opposite sides in both wars. Tennis took a back seat to winning the war. A year after the end of World War II, however, Davis Cup play resumed.

After the United States, the next most dominant country in Davis Cup play was Australia, with a total of 24 wins between 1900 and 1979. Arthur was keenly aware of this venerable tradition and of the prestige that was on the line every time his country played in an international arena. He was to discover, however, that among the younger generation of players, this tradition and its history meant absolutely nothing—and he would pay a steep price in trying to manage a team of tennis players who were distinct individuals, each with his own idea of right and wrong and not at all afraid to demand what he believed was right for him.

MANAGING THE "BAD BOYS"

Tony Trabert wanted out as Davis Cup captain in 1980 because he was sick and tired of dealing with the younger players, in particular because of their self-centeredness, their rudeness on the court, and their willingness to challenge the rules and traditions of tennis. Trabert was known as a tough "law-and-order" man when it came to enforcing discipline on the team. He was the captain, and the team was expected to follow his orders. The fact that many team members bucked his leadership was a source of great frustration.

Arthur also considered himself a law-and-order person, as long as the rules were fair, which in tennis he believed they were. But he thought his management of the team might be smoother because he could relate more easily to the younger generation of players since he was closer to them in age. He would soon discover, however, that this was not to be the case in all instances, that the job of managing the "bad boys" of tennis would be one of the most challenging times of his life.

Arthur was also taking over as captain at a time when Davis Cup play was losing its appeal around the world as a spectator sport. Many top players, not just some Americans, declined to play in Davis Cup matches, and attendance at Davis Cup games had dwindled over the years. Arthur felt that he had a responsibility to help restore Davis Cup play to its former esteem. In many countries, the Davis Cup squad is selected by a committee. But in the United States, the captain chooses the team, or, at least, extends the invitation to top players to join.

In 1980, Arthur already had some of the best young players on his team. One of the most talented—and one with a notorious reputation for bad behavior on court—was John McEnroe. Already on his way to becoming one of the greatest tennis players of all time, McEnroe was deeply committed to Davis Cup play. Jimmy Connors, however, was not, but despite his tiff with Arthur in the mid-1970s over his the question of his patriotism, he could be convinced to play Davis Cup tennis, although his commitment was never really strong or consistent. He had played a couple of Davis Cup matches in 1976 but had not been part of the team since then.

Soon after he took over as captain, however, Arthur had more on his mind than Connors. He had to assemble a team for a match against Mexico. For singles he had McEnroe and another fine player, Roscoe Tanner. His original doubles team, Stan Smith and Bob Lutz, was replaced by Marty Riessen and Sherwood Stewart after Smith developed an arm injury. McEnroe performed brilliantly, while the others on the team had their ups and downs. The United States won the games against Mexico, but the training sessions before the games and the games themselves were a quick initiation for Arthur into the difficulties of being captain. In dealing with the egos and demands of individuals who were used to being stars in their own right, having to "keep them happy"[3] was not a part of the job Arthur particularly liked. But he had to do it, and true to his well-developed sense of duty, he did.

The 1981 quarterfinal matches against the defending champion, Czechoslovakia, were played in the National Tennis Center in Flushing Meadows, Queens, New York, and they were an example of all the complex problems and frustrations Arthur faced as captain of the Davis Cup team. Arthur had assembled the strongest team possible: in addition to McEnroe, he had gotten the reluctant Connors to play, and Stan Smith and Bob Lutz were scheduled for the doubles match. The first match was between McEnroe and the rising Czech superstar Ivan Lendl. More than 17,000 fans bought tickets to see the two young stars play each other. The Davis Cup matches were suddenly a hot ticket for tennis fans who previously had not been interested.

Unfortunately for the U.S. team, McEnroe had just arrived from Wimbledon, where he had won the singles title, defeating Bjorn Borg of Sweden. But his behavior on court had been so volatile—he challenged line calls, cursed when things did not go his way, and pouted most of the time—that he was fined by the Wimbledon club and denied honorary membership in the club, which was routinely granted to all singles victors. The British fans were not in a forgiving mood; the day after the tournament, he was attacked in the British press. The entire experience was humiliating, although McEnroe had shown in the past that he had the ability to not be affected by the troubles brought on by his own bad behavior. In this instance, however, he was upset by what had happened at Wimbledon. Perhaps he understood that his antics at a place like Wimbledon reflected poorly on him and his country. When he went out on the court in New York, he had not yet recovered from the fiasco in Britain. The match against Lendl was played on a hot and humid day in July, and McEnroe was never able to get his serve going and to concentrate on Lendl, who was young and playing his best tennis. McEnroe lost in three straight sets—a bad defeat.

McEnroe's loss seemed to spur Connors on. The two were roughly the same age and were clear rivals on the court. Connors told the press that he didn't want the United States to lose another singles match, but Arthur suspected that, in addition, Connors would have welcomed winning in a tournament in which McEnroe had lost. Connors went on to defeat the Czech Tomas Smid. In the doubles, Smith and Lutz beat Lendl and Smid, and in the final singles matches, McEnroe beat Smid and Connors whipped Lendl. The matches turned out well in the end, but it was a hair-raising episode of hurt feelings and egotistical competition.

Arthur thought he had put together a solid team and even believed that Connors was now in the Davis Cup fold. He was wrong. Connors promised to play later in 1981, but he did not play another Davis Cup match for three years. He was clearly uneasy sharing the spotlight with McEnroe and was also not happy because he believed—rightly or wrongly—that McEnroe was allowed to "get away" with his bad behavior on court. (Connors apparently had forgotten about McEnroe's punishment and humiliation at Wimbledon.) Connors himself could show a hot temper on the court, but he never approached McEnroe's intensity and ability to offend the tennis establishment. McEnroe, brilliant and unpredictable, would continue to play great tennis but would try Arthur's patience at almost every turn.

In the finals in 1981 against Argentina, Arthur thought he and McEnroe might actually have a fist fight on the court. Arthur realized he could not coach McEnroe on tennis points—the young star knew what he wanted to do and how to do it and resisted all suggestions, even from another tennis great. McEnroe also was usually completely unremorseful over his bad behavior on court. In the final matches against Argentina, which were played in Cincinnati and which the United States would ultimately win, the audience included a large number of fans from Argentina who were there to root for their team. From the stands, some of them taunted McEnroe, as did members of the Argentine team. McEnroe began to lose his temper in one match and hurled curses at the audience and the Argentine players. Arthur stormed onto the court and told him to knock it off. McEnroe, as usual, answered back, and the two almost got into a fight. They didn't, probably because of Arthur's usual restraint, but it had been an unpleasant experience.

Despite these dramatics, the American team played brilliantly. Still, Arthur was furious and exhausted. The next day, he sat down and had a talk with McEnroe. It did not solve the problem, but it was important for Arthur to tell McEnroe what he felt and expected from him in a calmer environment than the tennis court. McEnroe listened in stony silence then left the room without saying a word. The two would never be close. McEnroe complained that Arthur was too remote and uninvolved as a coach, and Arthur would concede that when conflict arose, he often withdrew, not wanting to get involved in displays of emotion. But in this case, he had confronted McEnroe in a reasonable way and still had not gotten very far. It was a frustrating moment. Years after he had given up the captaincy of the Davis Cup team, Arthur reflected on his relationship with McEnroe. He realized that a part of him may actually have envied McEnroe's ability to express his rage, while Arthur had been trained so well not to show emotion, not to argue with bad calls, not to do anything to upset his opponent or the judges.

The 1982 Davis Cup season, unlike 1981, went off much more calmly. McEnroe, for whatever reason, was relatively calm on the court. The real fireworks turned out to be the competition itself. After beating India, the U.S. team went on to play Sweden in the quarterfinals in St. Louis, Missouri. Arthur had hoped that the matches against the Swedish team would not be difficult now that the great Bjorn Borg was no longer play-ing. But the Swedes put up a strong fight, and in the end, the winner would be decided by a match between McEnroe and the 17-year-old Mats Wilander, one of Sweden's hot young players. Wilander had just won the French Open and was emerging as one of the great young tennis stars. The match with McEnroe was a titanic struggle that lasted over 6 hours and went to 79 games before McEnroe finally one. Arthur rushed to greet McEnroe as he left the court. They embraced, and McEnroe wept with joy and exhaustion. Arthur later wrote that he had never admired McEnroe's mental stamina more than he did at that moment. The man, whatever his problems, was a true champion.

The semifinals of the 1982 David Cup were held in Australia, where once again McEnroe played brilliantly despite the jet lag everyone suffered because of the long flight from California. The U.S. team defeated the Australians in five straight games and then moved onto the finals, which were to be against the French team and played in Grenoble, France. Arthur was concerned about one player on the French team: the brilliant African-born Yannick Noah, now 22 years old. Arthur had seen him play as an 11-year-old in Africa and had predicted that he would grow up to be a great adult player. Noah put up a strong fight against McEnroe but in the end was defeated by the American in the fifth set. The U.S. team as a whole played brilliantly and won the finals, their second victory in a row. The French crowd had been particularly eager to see McEnroe, whom they found amusing. The atmosphere throughout the finals was friendly, and even though their team lost, the French seemed happy and gracious. After the U.S. victory, Arthur impressed the crowd by delivering his remarks in French, which he spoke fluently.

Arthur would serve as captain of the Davis Cup team for another three years, but there would not be another victory during his tenure. In 1984, Connors returned briefly to Davis Cup play, but in that year, both he and McEnroe behaved badly in the finals against Sweden, which the Swedes won. At the awards dinner, the president of the USTA apologized for the Americans' conduct. It was an indirect rebuke to Arthur as well. Criticism of his management of the team became more vocal, and some people even called for his resignation for failure to control Connors and McEnroe. Neither of them played in 1985, and the United States failed in that year to get to the finals, which were contested by Sweden and West Germany.

Arthur knew his days as Davis Cup captain were numbered. He had given it his best shot and secured two victories with talented but difficult players. For all the criticism that came his way because of McEnroe and Connors, in the end it would have been forgiven if the team had a string of victories. But the team was losing, and in October 1985, Arthur was removed as Davis Cup captain. The management of the U.S. Davis Cup effort wanted a fresh start with someone new, someone who might be better able to control and motivate the players and someone who could create a winning team. Arthur would have stayed on if he had been asked, but since he wasn't, he accepted their decision and prepared to move on to the next phase of his life. He knew full well that when one challenge ended, another opportunity would soon arise. He was tired—in no small part because once again, he had faced a health crisis.

HEART TROUBLE—AGAIN

In 1983, in the midst of his time as captain of the Davis Cup team, Arthur suffered a second heart attack. Early in that year, he had begun to feel ill. Chest pains had returned, and after extensive testing, his doctors recommended a double bypass operation. The news was devastating. Arthur had hoped that the first surgery in 1979 would correct the problem. Now he was told it had not and that he faced the same operation again, although this time involving two arteries, not four as in the first operation.

The second surgery, however, was more difficult than the first. The scar tissue in his chest bones made it more difficult for the surgeons to get at his heart. Also, for whatever reason, Arthur felt weaker than he had before the 1979 operation. The doctors determined that he had anemia—a low red blood cell count. To relieve his anemia, Arthur agreed to have a blood transfusion. He was given two pints of blood—and this blood transfusion would, as it was later discovered, be the cause of Arthur contracting AIDS. But that would not be known for several years. In 1983, while barely 40 years old, Arthur had already had two major heart operations. He was depressed and worried, but, as always, he picked himself up and carried on. When his captaincy of the Davis Cup team ended, Arthur looked forward to variety of new activities—as a businessman, a teacher, and a writer.

NOTES

1. Ashe, *Days of Grace,* p. 67.

2. For a more detailed discussion of Davis Cup rules and for a history of the competition, see the Davis Cup Web site at http://www.daviscup.com.

3. Ashe, *Days of Grace,* p. 77.

Arthur Ashe, the young champion. Ashe holds his trophy after winning the U.S. Open singles title in 1968. *(Courtesy of the International Tennis Hall of Fame)*

Davis Cup competition. Arthur Ashe plays a Davis Cup match. The Davis Cup trophy, in the foreground, stands ready for the victorious team. *(Courtesy of the International Tennis Hall of Fame)*

Defending champion. After winning the Wimbledon singles championship in 1975 at the age of 32, Arthur returned the following year to defend his title—unsuccessfully, as it turned out. He made it as far as the fourth round before being defeated. In this photo he plays a first-round match on June 22, 1976. (*Courtesy of Photofest*)

Managing the unmanageable. Arthur Ashe considered his captaincy of the Davis Cup team to be one of the hardest jobs he ever had because he had to manage young tennis players who often behaved badly on and off the court. Here, Jimmy Connors (right) addresses a press conference in New York City, while Arthur listens to John McEnroe, who strikes a characteristically cocky pose in shades. (*Courtesy of Photofest*)

Sports commentator. Arthur Ashe served as a TV sports commentator after his active career as a player was over. In this photo, he comments on ABC's "Tournament of Champions" in May 1980. (*Courtesy of Photofest*)

Arthur Ashe and his wife, Jeanne, at a masked ball early in their marriage. They were a highly popular couple on the social scene in New York, but they often preferred to spend quiet times at home. *(Courtesy of Photofest)*

Citizen of the world. A dramatic studio shot of Arthur taken in the latter part of his life. After his death, he was widely recognized not only as a tennis great, but as a humanitarian who helped raise awareness of apartheid and AIDS. (*Courtesy of Photofest*)

Chapter 6

BUSINESS AND EDUCATION

Throughout his years as captain of the Davis Cup team, Arthur maintained other interests in life. His busy schedule still allowed time to pursue things that had always fascinated him or that brought new challenges.

Arthur had majored in business when he attended college. His father was not a wealthy man, so he had grown up knowing the value of a dollar and the importance of not wasting anything. While he was a tennis player, he tended to be somewhat frugal. Players get much free clothing, for example, as part of promotional activities, so Arthur saved money by not having to buy a lot of clothing because of the free samples he was sometimes given. He never even owned his own car until 1986, not because he had no interest in cars, but because he was able to get around adequately without owning an automobile. Arthur was a risk taker on the tennis court, and, despite his frugality in personal matters, tended to be a risk taker in business ventures.

ARTHUR THE BUSINESSMAN

Arthur the businessman was a natural extension of Arthur the tennis player. A professional tennis career is over when one is still a relatively young person. Wise tennis players think ahead to the years when they are no longer on the court and will need income to live. As part of their planning, they hire business managers whose job is to advise them and manage their money.

Arthur's manager was his old friend Donald Dell, a lawyer and head of a sports-management company called ProServ, which specialized in representing tennis players and managing their financial and business affairs. Arthur had known the Dell family from Richmond days, and he had played on the Davis Cup team in 1968 and 1969 when Donald Dell was its captain. Dell was not only a manager but a trusted friend. Some of Arthur's African American friends criticized him for having a white manager and not turning that kind of business over to a black person or a black firm. Arthur countered by saying that there were no black sports managers when he started out, and in any event, the color of a person's skin was not the issue, but the trust you have in him. When it came to trust and friendship, Arthur had always been color blind.

At first, their relationship was informal, with Dell advising and managing Arthur's account without a contract. But in the mid-1980s, the federal government, for tax reasons and to prevent athletes from being cheated out of their money by unscrupulous advisors, required that written agreements exist between clients and their financial managers. Arthur, like other successful athletes, created a relationship under which he and Dell agreed on certain financial goals. Dell's job was to handle the details of meeting these objectives. Arthur was put on a budget based on his projected income. The rest of the money he earned was off limits to him. It was placed under the control of Dell, who invested it in Arthur's name.

The advantage of this arrangement was that Arthur did not have to deal with day-to-day financial worries. And, in some cases, he could be protected from making bad business decisions that could hurt him. Bills were paid by ProServ out of Arthur's money. Investment decisions were made by ProServ based on agreed-upon objectives. Presumably, good financial management would assure that Arthur would have substantial savings when he got older. In the meantime, he would have a hand in shaping the budget he lived on. Arthur had the right, of course, to go off on business ventures of his own, if he chose to do so, as long as he used the money in his personal budget. And on a number of occasions, he did.

Not all of these ambitious ventures proved successful. In 1979, Arthur and a friend from Richmond formed a trading company called International Commercial Resources. Donald Dell was opposed to the venture—he thought it was far too risky—but Arthur was determined to try his hand in forming a new company. Arthur and his partner had gone to Liberia, a nation in West Africa with historical ties to the United States, and signed agreements with the government to provide goods and services. Within a year, however, political and social chaos had descended on Liberia. The government was overthrown, civil war erupted, and one of the men Arthur and his partner had dealt with became a leader of the rebellion.

This man himself was murdered a number of years later. The venture collapsed, and Arthur and his partner lost hundreds of thousands of dollars.

Another business venture with his brother Johnnie, who was an officer in the Marines, also did not work out. Johnnie and Arthur came up with the idea of building an apartment complex in Jacksonville, North Carolina, to serve as housing for Marines stationed at the nearby Parris Island Marine base. For Arthur, the venture had special meaning because it gave him an opportunity to go into business with his younger brother. They decided to call the complex Cordell Village, after their late mother's birth name.

By 1990, however, Arthur and his brother realized they were in financial trouble. The rents on the apartments, which they had kept relatively low to accommodate the modest salaries of the Marines, were insufficient to cover the expenses of running the complex. Then in late 1990 and early 1991, the United States began sending thousands of troops overseas to fight in the Persian Gulf War. The war emptied Cordell Village as Marines gave up their apartments and were sent to the Saudi Arabia. Without tenants in their apartments, Arthur and Johnnie were losing money. They decided to sell the complex to the management agency that was operating it for them. Once again, Arthur lost hundreds of thousands of dollars.

Arthur was good-spirited about his losses, even though Dell and ProServ were less than pleased. Dell felt a responsibility to help Arthur save money and invest it wisely. He had approved Arthur's business ventures—reluctantly, as it turned out, and when the losses mounted, Dell was concerned. Arthur, as always, was a sensible person, and he was not the kind of person who would continue to make the same mistake over and over. Although he was fascinated with business ventures, Arthur realized that he was better off being a consultant or a spokesman for business.[1]

ARTHUR THE SPOKESMAN AND EDUCATOR

Arthur was an excellent spokesman—both for products and for causes. As a world-famous athlete, he was asked continually to endorse products. And product endorsement is always a good source of income. It is a tempting opportunity for athletes, who often endorse such diverse products as sneakers and other athletic clothing, soft drinks, or even automobiles. Philosophically, Arthur had no problem being a spokesman for certain products of American enterprise. He believed in the American economic system and in the rewards it could bring to anyone who worked hard. In the course of his life, he endorsed a number of products, but the ones he was most associated with were produced by Head USA, a company that manufactured tennis and ski equipment and clothing. At various times he also worked for the car manufacturer Volvo, for the clothing manufacturer Le Coq Sportif, and for Philip Morris, although he did not endorse any of that company's tobacco products.

Arthur was conflicted about working for Philip Morris. Even though it was a diversified company that produced many different things, its main product was cigarettes, and the connection between smoking and lung and heart disease was clear. Nevertheless, tobacco companies had given much money in support of the sport of tennis. The first sponsor of the U.S. Open was Marlboro cigarettes, and the Virginia Slims brand hosted a well-known professional tournament for women. Because of Philip Morris's generosity to the game of tennis, Arthur was willing to associate himself with the company's non-tobacco products only. Arthur also served as a consultant and occasional columnist for *Tennis* magazine. All of these connections earned income for Arthur, but they also represented connections to companies and the people who worked in them, and he valued the friendships he made in the course of his work with corporate America.

In his later life, Arthur often commented on how much he liked working for the Aetna Life and Casualty Company, the giant insurance and financial services company located in Connecticut. Arthur first came into contact with Aetna in the early 1970s, when it began to sponsor a professional tennis competition called the World Cup. After each World Cup tournament, the Aetna executives would host a dinner for the participants. In the course of these dinners, Arthur came to know the president of Aetna, William Bailey, and was deeply impressed by Bailey's interest in social issues, especially health care.

In the late 1970s, Aetna hired Arthur as a consultant on "racial issues." Like many large companies at that time, Aetna was determined to recruit talented African Americans for its workforce in order to create a more diversified workplace and to have more black people in executive positions. As an unpaid consultant, Arthur advised Aetna on hiring policies and on how to recruit talented black men and women. In 1982, Bailey, greatly impressed with Arthur's work as a consultant and with his superior intelligence, asked him to become a member of the company's board of directors. This was an enormous step for Arthur. Being a consultant was an advisory position. Being a member of the board, however, meant that we would vote on company policy, helping set the direction of a multibillion-dollar company.

At first, Arthur had concerns about joining the board. He was only the second African American to sit on the board, and he worried that he was chosen to be a "token" black. Bailey, however, reassured Arthur by telling him that as a board member he should feel free to ask any question, state any point of view, and take his position seriously. When he joined the Aetna board, Arthur assumed he would be a kind of spokesman in the company for blacks and for issues relating to race. His experience on the board, however, was that he became most influential—because of his own illnesses—on health care issues. Because Aetna was in the insurance business, Arthur became aware of how many Americans did not have health insurance and received inferior medical care, or in many cases, no medical care at all. Health care for all Americans would remain one of his primary concerns throughout his life, and his interest in and knowledge of the issue stemmed from his work on the Aetna board.

Arthur did not escape criticism for his association with Aetna. During his time on the board of directors, the company decided to stop selling individual health-insurance policies. The company was losing money on policies sold to individuals. What it did best, and made money on, was group insurance; that is, insurance policies sold to other companies who would make them available to their employees as part of their benefits package. Arthur voted to end Aetna's sale of individual policies—he felt this was good business and made sense. But he and the company were criticized for the move. Arthur always believed it was the right decision. As a board member, he had taken on a responsibility for the company's financial well-being, and in that spirit, he supported business decisions that enabled the company to prosper.

Arthur brought a voice for racial minorities and the poor onto the Aetna board of directors, but he also brought the voice of the ailing—and in his case, the voice of a sufferer of heart disease and AIDS, although it wasn't until 1992 that most of the other board members found out Arthur had AIDS.[2]

Arthur the spokesman was also active in promoting social issues in the United States that mattered to him, through special organizations designed to help people. He had become involved in American social causes while still playing tennis, but after his retirement, the pace of his commitments increased. As part of his interest in promoting social welfare, Arthur helped found a number of organizations. One that was particularly close to his heart was the Ashe-Bollettieri Cities program, known as ABC for short. The idea came to Arthur and his friend Nick Bollettieri when they were attending the French Open tournament in Paris in 1987. Bollettieri was one of the great tennis coaches in the United States and the owner of the Bollettieri Tennis Academy in Bradenton, Florida. He had been the coach to many champions, including Andre Agassi and Monica Seles, both Grand Slam tournaments winners.

Ashe and Bollettieri were discussing one day the plague of crime and violence in American cities. As a result of their discussions, they decided they should do something to help the youth of the United States who were less fortunate than they were. In 1988 they founded ABC. Its goal was to go into the inner cities and select talented kids who would be good candidates to attend the Bollettieri Academy, where they would be exposed not only to tennis but to other positive influences. The program's first participants came from Newark, New Jersey, which had a large African American population and many poor neighborhoods. These were young girls and boys who had little if any exposure to tennis but who showed promise and the ability to learn and grow.

The ABC program was a noble idea, but it soon ran into problems with money, and for a while, Bollettieri contributed funds from the Academy to cover the costs of ABC. That situation could not go on indefinitely, however. The program had been conceived initially as a partnership between the Bollettieri Academy and the government of the cities where the participating children lived. The city governments helped select the children who were sent into the program. As part of the partnership, city government had promised financial support, but getting money out of government bureaucracies proved almost impossible, even though the promises had been made. Because local governments faced severe financial strains in the 1980s, the funds for the ABC program were often delayed or never materialized in the end. When faced with the need to pay their police and fire officers, local governments chose those kinds of needs over any contributions to a tennis program.

Eventually, Bollettieri could no longer afford to personally underwrite the effort and was forced to pull out of ABC. Arthur decided to place direction of the program under another organization he had founded, Athletes Career Connection (ACC). Arthur had founded ACC after reading a disturbing statistic: only one in four African American athletes in football and basketball in Division One schools (the top sporting colleges in the United States) was graduating from college. Arthur hoped that ACC would be a program that successfully motivated black students to take their studies seriously. By mentoring African American students, the program was designed for them to improve their academic scores while they pursued their interests in athletics. The weakness in ACC, as in ABC, turned out to be money, since it needed the financial support of the college where the program operated. In 1990, during an economic recession, the money dried up, and the ACC went out of business. As was the case with ABC, the ACC was not a high funding priority when money was in scarce supply.

These financial difficulties did not cause Arthur to give up on his support of educational issues. He had always stressed the importance of athletes getting a good all-around education. Arthur's efforts in this direction were part of the Safe Passage Foundation, another nonprofit group he created to help poor kids make the transition from childhood to adulthood. Safe Passage was fortunate to get some generous corporate sponsors, including the Nestlé company, which in 1992 gave Safe Passage a grant of $100,000. By the early 1990s, Safe Passage had more than 1,000 kids enrolled just in Newark, where it ran tennis programs, including one for very young kids that was called the "tiny tots tennis program."

Through Safe Passage and the other programs he established, Arthur relentlessly hammered home the importance of getting a good education. As late as 1992, less than a year before his death and when other causes were consuming much of his time and efforts, Arthur continued to stress the importance of education for African American athletes. In that year he founded and served as chairman of African American Athletic Association (AAAA), yet another organization dedicated to mentoring young black athletes. In addition to counseling and advising young student-athletes, the AAAA also worked to create job opportunities for them and to shape public policy by doing research in the area of sports and education.[3]

When it came to education, Arthur was definitely a traditionalist: he believed in education, and he believed it mattered very much that black boys and girls go to school, learn as much as they could, and graduate from high school and college. This belief often placed him at odds with other leaders in the black community, especially in the 1970s. Leaders of the "Black Power" movement sometimes denigrated traditional education, which they saw as a white man's tool for retaining power and control over blacks. In the 1980s, some radical black academics became faculty members at prestigious universities, where they used their influence to belittle what they called "white" education.

Arthur was strongly opposed to these trends and to what he considered the educational bias of the Black Power movement. He was not a fan of such Black Power leaders as Stokely Carmichael or H. Rap Brown. Nor did he respond favorably to the message of Malcolm X, who preached black self-reliance (which Arthur approved of) but also a kind of black separatism that Arthur found objectionable. These men, in his opinion, were dividing the country and in the end not really helping the black family. He looked at the deterioration of the black family in America—the low graduation rates from school, the poverty and crime, the increasing numbers of unmarried teenage mothers—and he was deeply upset.

His efforts to help reverse these negative trends were rooted in traditional solutions, in a profound belief in the importance of education as a means for overcoming social ills. The black leaders he admired most were people who had received a good education, overcome the poverty they were raised in, and gone on to have distinguished careers in their fields. Men like Andrew Young, Gov. L. Douglas Wilder of Virginia, Rep. Maxine Waters of California, the Rev. Jesse Jackson, and Mayor Maynard Jackson of Atlanta were all, in Arthur's view, "role models" for young black people. They respected traditional values and believed that black people were part of America and needed to be integrated more into American life. But among those who disagreed with him, Arthur realized, "I hardly count."[4] Arthur believed in cooperation, integration, and harmony among the races. Anyone who preached otherwise was, to him, someone who was actually hurting black people.

Arthur's interest in education extended briefly into the area of teaching. In 1983 he was invited to give a lecture at Yale University as part of the Kiphuth Fellowship, named after a longtime swimming coach at the university. The subject Arthur chose to speak on was "College Athletics: A Reappraisal." As a result of this lecture, which was highly regarded, Arthur was invited to teach at Yale. It was a great honor, and he felt he was up to the task. But after some reflection, he decided to decline the offer. Yale, with its exceptionally talented student body and it ample resources, was not a place where Arthur felt he could be most useful. When the opportunity arose again to teach, Arthur decided to accept an offer to teach a course at Florida Memorial College, a black school that was not too far from the Doral Club in Miami, where Arthur was still the director of the tennis program. Already on the board of trustees of the school, Arthur now had a welcome opportunity to interact with the students, who came from middle-class and poor families. Arthur was asked to teach a course called The Black Athlete in Contemporary Society.

The course was attended by about 12 students, a comfortable number that allowed Arthur to get to know each one individually and to learn about their abilities and weaknesses. The students were all bright and eager. But when Arthur read their first papers, he was shocked. The majority of the students had very weak writing skills. They were poor spellers and had no sense of organization or logic in the presentation of their subjects. Arthur was depressed and angry. This was not college-level work. These students would soon have to enter the real world, where their skills would be woefully inadequate, making it all the more difficult for them to find and hold down good, well-paying jobs.

One thing that Arthur was adamant about was the need for college administrators to hold their athletes to high academic standards—a position that was not popular with many schools or students. Many colleges with active athletic programs often offered scholarships to outstanding young high school athletes. If their academic performances were below standard, the colleges often looked the other way and allowed the student to pass through, despite failing grades: such was the importance of athletics. The system that put athletics first and academics second was deeply ingrained in many schools in the United States.

This kind of conveyor-belt education, in which learning was in essence sacrificed to the needs of the colleges' athletic programs, was not unique to black colleges. But, from Arthur's point of view, the problem in black institutions was especially severe. Many African American college students, because of poverty and inadequate primary education, arrived in college lacking basic skills necessary for college work. Such students, in Arthur's opinion, were not being helped by being given a "pass" on academics simply because they were good on the basketball court or the football field. In fact, they were being used by the schools to bolster their athletic programs.

The National Collegiate Athletic Association (NCAA), which governs college athletics, proposed in the 1980s that higher academic standards be required for freshmen before they were eligible to play collegiate athletics. Scholarships could be awarded, but if a student fell below standards, he or she would not be allowed to play until academic performance improved. Arthur backed the proposed changes 100 percent. But he came up against the opposition of many prominent African American individuals and organizations, including the Rev. Jesse Jackson and the National Association for the Advancement of Colored People (NAACP), who felt that the changes were discriminatory. Arthur held his ground and even published an essay titled "Coddling the Black Athlete," in which he deplored the lack of academic standards for black athletes. He received a lot of criticism for his point of view, but he never changed it. Arthur truly believed that black athletes needed to be treated like other students and held to the high standards that were necessary to graduate from college.

ARTHUR THE WRITER

In the course of his teaching and work with college students, Arthur became aware of the fact that very little written material existed on the African American athlete. Blacks were disproportionately represented in such sports as boxing, baseball, basketball, and track, to name just a few.

Yet almost nothing had ever been written about them. One could find an occasional biography of a famous black athlete, usually someone, like Jackie Robinson, who had been successful in an integrated sport and had received national recognition. But nothing had been written about African American athletes as a whole. No scholarly study existed of the historic contribution to sports that the black athlete had made over the centuries.

Arthur was mystified by this lack of information. The more he thought about it, the more he felt, in his own words, "a burning sense of obligation" to do something about it.[5] Arthur decided to do the research and write a history of the African American athlete. Having written before, he knew the procedures—and difficulties—required to find a publisher. He had a lot of positives to offer when pursuing a book project. He was famous, he had written before, and the subject he had chosen had not been covered before, at least to the extent he wanted to cover it. But it was still an effort to get the project off the ground. Rather than begging for money from a publisher, Arthur decided at the outset to pay for the cost of researching and writing the manuscript out of his own pocket. That way, he had more control over the project and could do it on his own terms.

He hired a staff, which included a typist to prepare the manuscript and keep the files, and researchers to help gather all the information. They included Sandra Jamison, a librarian, Rodney Howard, a talented young researcher, Francis Harris, who handled the reference sections, and Professor Kip Branch of Wilson College, who edited Arthur's original prose. In all the project took some five years to pull together and cost Arthur more than $300,000 of his own money.

Getting the book into print was also a difficult process. A finished manuscript needed to be typeset, printed, and bound in order to be a publishable, sellable book. Arthur decided to sign a contract for the book's production with Howard University Press and its executive director, Charles F. Harris. Arthur had come to Howard, a black university, after some twenty commercial publishers had turned down the proposal, believing that a history of the black athlete in the United States would not sell enough to warrant publication. A university press, however— a nonprofit publishing enterprise—is committed to publishing worthwhile works of scholarship regardless of their commercial possibilities. At least that is how it is supposed to work.

In late 1985, Charles Harris left Howard University Press, and a few months later, the company informed Arthur that it was no longer interested in the project. By this time, some 75 percent of the work had been completed. It had to go on. After leaving Howard, Harris was attempting to form his own publishing company, Amistad Press, which was to be owned and operated by African Americans and committed to publishing African American authors. Harris was still very much interested in the project. (Amistad Press was named after the infamous slave ship in the nineteenth century.)

Seeking another publisher to assist with the costs of the book, Harris and Arthur approached Dodd, Mead, a distinguished publishing company with a history of publishing black authors. A contract was signed in August 1986 to bring out Arthur's work as a joint venture between Amistad Press and Dodd, Mead. In early 1988, however, Dodd, Mead fell into financial difficulties and could no longer commit to the project. Harris then turned to Warner Books, a subsidiary of the communications giant Warner Communications. A new contract was signed, and the book was finally published in the fall of 1988.

Arthur had no regrets about the difficult process in finding a copublisher to produce the book, nor did he regret the amount of time, energy, and money he had sunk into the project. When it was finished, he had created a monumental three-volume history of the African American athlete that covered the years 1619 to the mid-1980s. Entitled *A Hard Road to Glory*, it is still regarded as the definitive history of African Americans in sports. When the first books came off the press, they arrived at Harris's home. He asked Arthur to come over to see them. He later described Arthur's reaction: "He simply stared at them. We both looked at each other and smiled continuously.... I think we were all nearly speechless because we realized what a tremendous ordeal and success we had experienced together."[6]

Arthur had written a number of works in his life, but nothing approached the pride he felt with the publication of *A Hard Road to Glory*. It was definitely one of the great achievements of his life, a monument that would remain for years to come.

NOTES

1. Ashe, *Days of Grace*, pp. 202–206.

2. See ibid., pp. 206–213, for Arthur's views about his relationship with Aetna.

3. Ibid., pp. 285–287.

4. Ibid., p. 172.

5. Ibid., p. 192.

6. Harris recounts the difficulties in getting the project published in Ashe, Arthur, Jr., *A Hard Road to Glory: The African-American in Track and Field* (New York: Amistad Press, 1993), pp. ix–xi. This work is one of five spin-offs from the massive three-volume work that are devoted to specific sports. In addition to the one cited here on track and field, there are separate volumes covering baseball, basketball, boxing, and football.

Chapter 7

TRAGEDY AND TRIUMPH

Arthur Ashe's life had been blessed. He had risen to the top of the tennis world, winning some of the most coveted trophies. He was among the most beloved players in the game, in no small part because of his character and calm and dignified personality. He had also begun to lend his name to worthy social causes, such as the fight against apartheid in South Africa and the improvement of education among young African Americans. And he had begun a happy and successful marriage in his 30s. But, clouding all this happiness and achievement was a stark and unexpected reality: He had suffered health problems at an early age. Most men do not expect to have a heart attack at the age of 36, especially someone who is in great shape and is a professional athlete. Yet, Arthur had undergone two heart surgeries. He seemed to have triumphed over this adversity, and he accepted the fact that he could no longer play professional tennis and threw himself into a variety of activities that utilized his many talents in business and for the betterment of people who were less fortunate than he. And he was blessed with another joy in life—a baby daughter.

CAMERA

Arthur and Jeanne waited nine years before starting a family. They both loved children and wanted to have a family, but each realized that many things had to be considered before bringing a child into the world. For one, Arthur and Jeanne were both deeply involved in their careers. They understood a child would need to have their undivided attention, so they hesitated in the early years of their marriage and chose not to start a family right away. Arthur was still active in the tennis world, and Jeanne was busy pursuing her career as a photographer.

The most important issue influencing Jeanne and Arthur's decision whether or not to start a family was the question of health—both Arthur's and their respective families'. Heart disease ran in his family, and the child of a parent with this condition is at high risk of developing heart disease as well. In addition, heart disease was a severe problem in Jeanne's family. A younger brother had died of a heart attack at an early age. Any child of Arthur and Jeanne's would therefore be in a higher category of risk for having heart problems. The thought of creating a child who would face, at the very least, a high risk of heart disease caused Arthur and Jeanne to stop and think carefully about their options.

But as the years went by, both Arthur and Jeanne realized that they wanted to be parents. After much consideration, they decided there was a way they could have a child: they could adopt. This choice would allow them to be loving parents to a child in need of a family, and it would remove the fear they had of having a child of their own who would be susceptible to illnesses that were risk factors in their genetic makeup. In December 1986, after nine years of marriage, the Ashes adopted a baby girl, and they named her Camera. The name may have seemed somewhat unusual, but it obviously had an association with photography, Jeanne's profession. But Arthur and Jeanne also thought the name had a pretty sound to it. In preparation for bringing a child into their lives, Arthur and Jeanne decided to move out of Manhattan. They purchased a house and piece of land in Mount Kisco, in Westchester County, just north of the city. Camera would have the advantages of growing up close to New York City, with all its cultural life and big-city entertainment and excitement. And, by living in the suburbs, she could also enjoy a beautiful home with green grass and the surrounding forests and, when it came time, the excellent schools that the county offered.

Becoming a father changed Arthur. Everyone who knew him commented on it. His focus was now on his family, his daughter, on being a good father, and on considering everything from the perspective of how it would affect Camera. He enjoyed the day-to-day activities of raising a child and eagerly did his share as a father, which included feeding, changing diapers, and spending time with the baby. He was happy in a way he had never been before. That happiness would soon be tempered by devastating news.

AIDS

Camera was not even two years old when something went wrong in Arthur's body. He did not feel well. He and Jeanne and Camera were enjoying a weekend at Lake George, New York, in August 1988 when Arthur began to notice a problem with his right hand. At first, he had trouble when trying to use a telephone. He just could not get his fingers to work. He told Jeanne, who thought maybe Arthur had cut off circulation in his hand by sleeping on it. The problem, however, was not numbness—which would go away shortly after you got out of bed and once circulation returned—but the inability to use his hand at all.

Arthur decided to wait a day to see if his hand would improve. But by the next day, his hand was even more incapacitated, hanging totally useless at his side. This was obviously something more serious than a circulatory problem. Arthur wondered if he had had a stroke. Having had a heart attack at 36, he would not have been surprised at all if such a serious illness hit him in his mid-40s. There was only one way to find out what was wrong. He made an appointment with his doctor in Mount Kisco. Before seeing him, however, Arthur and Jeanne had to do a live TV interview. During the interview, Arthur successfully hid his paralyzed hand. No one who saw the interview was aware that he could not move it.

After the interview, Arthur and Jeanne drove down to see his physician, Dr. William Russell, at the Mount Kisco Medical Group in Westchester County. Dr. Russell, an older man with a calm and friendly manner, was concerned about Arthur's condition and said that he needed to have a scan of his brain done immediately. The scan, as Dr. Russell had feared, revealed something that looked like a patch on Arthur's brain. He needed to be evaluated as soon as possible by a neurologist. Whatever this patch was, it was likely to be causing the paralysis in Arthur's hand.

Arthur went immediately to New York Hospital in Manhattan, where he was evaluated by Dr. John Caronna, a neurologist. Dr. Caronna suggested that an exploratory operation be performed to determine the exact nature of the abnormality on Arthur's brain. Before making a final decision on an operation, Arthur consulted with two other doctors, and they agreed that an operation was the best possible option. Brain scans and conventional X-rays could not determine the exact nature of the lesion that was on Arthur's brain. The doctors would have to go in, take out the patch, and examine it under a microscope. The only other choice was to do nothing and see if his condition worsened, but this was not acceptable to Arthur. He needed both hands.

Before the surgery was performed, Arthur underwent a series of blood tests. These tests revealed further devastating news: Arthur was suffering from the human immunodeficiency virus (HIV) in his blood. He was HIV positive. He had been infected with the virus that causes the disease acquired immunodeficiency syndrome (AIDS). The most likely source of the infection was a tainted blood transfusion that Arthur had received after his second heart bypass operation in 1983. Today, all blood used for transfusions is tested to make sure it is not infected with the HIV virus. In 1983, however, such a test did not exist. A patient receiving a blood transfusion could only hope that the blood he or she was receiving was free of contamination. Arthur had had the bad luck of getting two pints of blood that were infected with the virus that causes AIDS. There was no other explanation. By 1985, a test that could be applied to all blood donated to blood banks had been developed to detect the presence of the HIV virus. Before then, the Centers for Disease Control in Atlanta, which monitors disease and illnesses in the United States, estimated that 13,000 Americans contracted HIV infection from having tainted blood transfusion.[1]

On September 8, 1988, Arthur underwent an exploratory brain operation. The doctors found an infection and cleared it out. In recovery immediately after the surgery, Arthur was amazed that the brain operation was a lot less painful than heart surgery. In fact, he experienced very little discomfort at all. But when the results of the test on the infection that had been removed came back, the news, while not totally surprising, was shocking. The infection was called toxoplasmosis, a rare bacterial infection of the brain that was one of the conditions associated with AIDS. Arthur was not only HIV positive. He had full-blown AIDS.[2]

"MAKE THE BEST OF THE SITUATION"

Arthur took the news of his illness calmly and with little show of emotion. That was the only way he knew how to deal with crises. He said he would "make the best of the situation."[3] Today, medicine has made enormous strides in the treatment of AIDS. The illness is not curable, but in the early twenty-first century, many people with AIDS live with and manage their disease through a combination of sophisticated drugs. But in the late 1980s, these treatments had not yet been developed. An infection like toxoplasmosis, once diagnosed, could be treated with antibiotics and cleared up—as happened with Arthur. Toxoplasmosis, while a serious illness, was almost never fatal to AIDS patients. It could be treated.

But AIDS patients were susceptible to a variety of other ailments that were life threatening, such as Kaposi's sarcoma (called KS for short), a rare skin cancer, several types of pneumonia, "wasting disease" (in which one steadily loses weight and becomes skeleton-like in appearance), plus such torments as thrush (a bacterial infection that leaves the tongue and throat coated with a white substance), meningitis, tuberculosis, and even dementia. Each ailment could be treated individually, but eventually, as the body's immune system collapsed under the assault of the virus and other infections, the AIDS sufferer became more and more susceptible to one disease after another and would eventually die. In 1988, when Arthur was diagnosed, the prognosis for a person with AIDS was not good. Medications that treated the virus itself had not been developed. All a person could do was to hope that he or she would avoid a life-threatening infection and that the immune system would hold out for as long as possible. But most AIDS patients rarely survived more than five years after diagnosis.

There was another aspect of AIDS that made it an especially difficult illness to bear. When AIDS first became a national health issue in the early 1980s, the public came to associate it as a disease of gay men and intravenous drug addicts (those who used needles to inject their drugs). While it is true that AIDS was first noticed in the gay male community— and that it can be transmitted through unprotected sexual relations—it was, as a disease, more complicated than being simply a sexually transmitted ailment. Nor was it only a disease of drug addicts who passed on the infection by using unclean needles that transmitted minute blood products from one person to the other. But in the public mind in these early years, AIDS was the "gay disease" or the "drug addicts' disease." It was an unfair simplification of a complex medical problem. There was much that was not known about AIDS in the 1980s. Even today, decades after the disease was first discovered, its origins and all the ways it may be spread are still not fully understood. For example, many millions of people in Africa are afflicted with the ailment, which is a genuine scourge to the continent and a threat to the very existence of populations in many countries. Africans with AIDS are not all gay, nor are they all intravenous drug users. In other words, the stigma associated with AIDS in the United States was unfair and made life for those suffering from the illness even more unbearable.

For Arthur, a person who had always cared deeply about his reputation (he wrote in 1992 that "I want no stain on my character, no blemish on my reputation."[4]), the stigma associated with AIDS was a heart-breaking burden. In addition, Arthur was a person who believed deeply in the right to privacy, even if one was a celebrity. Immediately after his diagnosis, Arthur and Jeanne had to consider whom to tell. Arthur was grateful that Camera, not yet two years old, was too young to understand his condition, although as she got older, she would have to be told. Arthur, as a public figure, was particularly concerned that he and Jeanne control the information about his illness. Obviously, certain hospital staff knew—they had worked on his case, handled his files, and done the lab work on his blood. Arthur was well aware that sensational tabloid newspapers often paid people who worked in hospitals for gossip about celebrities. And he knew that as soon as the world knew, everyone would ask, "How had Arthur Ashe become infected?" "Is he gay?" "Is he a drug user?"

He was terribly afraid that his loved ones would one day pick up a news tabloid and read that he had AIDS. He was sure that he could never tell his father, whose heart was weak from several heart attacks and who was in declining health. For Arthur, the reality set in immediately. "From the days I found out that I had AIDS, I have had to live with the knowledge that my days are numbered," he wrote in 1992.[5] Yet, he refused to have anything but a positive attitude. "One simply must not despair, not even for a moment,"[6] he later wrote. His first concern, not surprisingly, was for Jeanne and Camera. Could he have somehow infected them? That was a thought that was too much to bear. Both Jeanne and Camera were tested immediately and were found not to have the HIV virus. Arthur was immensely relieved, but both Jeanne and Camera would need to be tested on a regular basis for the next few years just to make sure that the virus was not lurking within them.

Shortly after his AIDS diagnosis, Arthur developed a number of physical problems that were painful but treatable. Since he was allergic to the antibiotic penicillin, he was given a sulfur-based drug which, for some reason, crystallized in his system and created kidney stones. He suffered excruciating back pain until this condition was corrected. Then he came down with a condition called Stevens-Johnson Syndrome, which left his body looking as if it had been severely burned. This, too, was corrected by medication, but Arthur's skin never looked healthy again.

A PARTNER IN TREATMENT

Arthur believed passionately that he personally had to be closely involved in his treatment. He needed to seek out the best doctors, and he needed not to be afraid to ask questions and become involved. He knew that patients who take an active partnership with their doctors in their treatment are far better off—they are less likely to become depressed and often live longer than patients, regardless of their disease, who sit back and do nothing.

Arthur realized he had become a professional patient. Much of the rest of his life would be spent visiting doctors. Because of his dual conditions—heart problems and AIDS—he had many doctors and would be required to take many pills. The doctors would have to coordinate with each other and make sure that the different medications did not conflict with each other and poison Arthur. At one point, Arthur was taking a staggering 30 pills a day. This, as it turns out, is not unusual for AIDS patients. Five of his medications were for his heart condition, and the remainder were for AIDS.

AIDS treatment was in its early days at the time Arthur was diagnosed. Most AIDS patients could have only their symptoms treated. But in 1987, a new drug, called azidothymidine, or AZT for short, was rushed onto the market. It was an antiviral agent, which meant it was believed that it could attack the underlying condition of AIDS—the HIV virus. AZT did not go through all the testing trials usually required for a drug. There were immense pressures on the government to approve the drug to help AIDS sufferers and to skip over the years-long testing procedures. Many people with AIDS were willing to take the risks and use AZT without the results of the long experiments and tests that usually precede the approval of medications, so desperate were they for some kind of relief.

As a result, much was not known about AZT as it began to be used—what were the best dosages, what were its long-term effects, did it really help at all? Today, AZT is part of a package of drugs used to treat AIDS patients. In 1988, it was the only antiviral agent. And in its early use, doctors tended to prescribe it in dosages that were very high compared with how it is used today. Arthur began by taking 10 capsules a day. By 1992, he had been reduced to three capsules a day. AZT killed the HIV virus, but it was like killing a mosquito with a hammer: it also killed healthy cells and had to be considered toxic. Some doctors thought it was so poisonous that it was life threatening to weaker AIDS patients. Arthur knew about the debate that swirled around AZT, but he chose to take it anyway. He had been active in his treatment plan, and he had made the decision and refused to dwell on whether or not the higher doses he took in 1988 and 1989 had damaged his body.

As he was adjusting to living with AIDS, Arthur had to face one of the greatest sadnesses in his life. In March 1989, he, Jeanne, and Camera were relaxing at their home in Florida, at the Doral Resort and Country Club. On March 19, the phone rang. Jeanne answered. It was Arthur's stepsister, Loretta. She was calling to tell them that Arthur's father had died of a stroke while at her home near Richmond. Arthur wept when he heard the news. His father had always been there to protect and guide him. He had been present at Arthur's greatest tennis triumphs, including the U.S. Open and Wimbledon. And he had lived to see Arthur and Jeanne become parents. Now he was gone. Arthur had worried about protecting *him* from the news that his beloved son had AIDS. Now that anxiety was gone. His father had gone to his grave never knowing about Arthur's illness.

Arthur had told only a few people he trusted about his illness. He was able to maintain control over that information for three-and-a-half years. In 1992, however, all that would change suddenly.

NOTES

1. Ashe, *Days of Grace*, pp. 231–232.
2. Ibid., pp. 218–226.
3. Ibid., p. 226.
4. Ibid., p. 4.
5. Ibid., p. 229.
6. Ibid., p. 233.

Chapter 8

THE FINAL YEAR

Arthur always believed that public figures, people in the news, whether in sports, politics, or entertainment were entitled to their privacy, especially when it came to such personal matters as issues of health. From 1988 until 1992 he was able to keep his AIDS status private, although he was always very much aware that rumors surfaced from time to time about his condition. These rumors were fueled by his physical appearance: he was extremely thin, and, in truth, he did not look healthy. In some respects, any unhealthy appearance could easily be attributed to his heart condition, and, in fact, his heart problems may have acted as a shield from reporters getting at the underlying cause, which was AIDS. Arthur chose to ignore the rumors concerning his health that were swirling about him, and he went about his business, hoping that his medical condition would remain private and not become the subject of public speculation or knowledge. But in 1992, his hopes were dashed, and in a matter of hours, his world came crashing down around him. The web of secrecy and privacy that he had constructed to protect himself, Jeanne, and Camera was penetrated, to his dismay and anger.

THE ANNOUNCEMENT

On April 7, 1992, Arthur got a phone call from an old friend, Doug Smith, at the time a tennis writer with the newspaper USA Today. As Doug started to speak, Arthur could tell that he was clearly uncomfortable in the conversation. What he said was devastating. He told Arthur that the newspaper had a lead it was investigating that Arthur was HIV positive and might even have AIDS. Arthur remained calm, but he refused to confirm or deny the rumor. His anger rising, he asked to speak with Doug's boss, Gene Policinski. Policinski, the managing editor for sports, called Arthur back and asked the same question that Doug had asked: Do you have AIDS? Again, Arthur refused to confirm or deny that he was ill with the disease, but he firmly insisted that he was no longer a public figure and that his health problems were his business and not the public's. Policinski politely disagreed. He reminded Arthur that he was indeed still a public figure, and that the health of any public figure is a legitimate story—as had been his hearts attack in 1979 and his surgeries in 1979 and 1983. As a journalist, Policinski was right, but Arthur could not see it that way.

Arthur was smart enough to realize that he had lost the match—it was now just a matter of time before his secret was known to the whole world. Still refusing to answer yes or no to the question, Arthur asked for 36 hours before the paper printed anything. Policinski refused, but he told Arthur that they had not completed their background investigation and would not publish anything until then. Arthur canceled his schedule for the day, which had included a trip to Washington, to sit down with Jeanne and decide what their next step should be. They had always known deep down that the news would eventually come out, but now they were faced with the reality. They had to act immediately. Arthur and Jeanne realized that the worst thing would be to do nothing and to wake up tomorrow or the day after and see a headline "Arthur Ashe has AIDS" splashed across the front of a newspaper, or, even worse, to turn on the TV and see his medical condition a top story on the national news.

After weighing their options, Arthur and Jeanne decided to hold a news conference the next day at which he would tell the world that he had AIDS. It was a monumental step—one that went against every grain of his beliefs. In the end, Arthur could never give up the belief that he should not have to go public with such personal information. Now he was forced to, and it seemed so unjust. He had been a good person all his life; why should be denied the basic right of privacy? And he was seething with anger.[1] In 1989, very few public figures who had AIDS went public with the information. There was still a great stigma attached to the disease. Magic Johnson, the famous basketball player, had revealed in November 1988 that he was HIV positive, but he was one of the few exceptions. The movie star Rock Hudson admitted he had AIDS only days before he died. The ballet star Rudolf Nureyev had died of AIDS and demanded that his doctor deny he had AIDS even after his death. Magic Johnson said he had contracted AIDS through unprotected heterosexual sex. Hudson and Nureyev were widely believed to be homosexual, but neither had ever discussed that they had AIDS, never mind whether that it came from sexual contact with other men.

Arthur wondered what his life would be like after the announcement. Would people think he had contracted the disease through the use of dirty needles or through gay sex? Would he be allowed to go to Wimbledon, or would be banned from traveling to Britain? Some countries would not let AIDS patients in, including South Africa, which Arthur had traveled to in 1991. At that time, he had lied on his entry visa application—not admitting that he had the disease—in order to be allowed in the country. His mind raced, imagining all kinds of situations and possibilities, none of them good. Throughout his life, his reputation had always meant so much to him. Now it seemed to be ripped from his control and about to be dashed in the mud, with strangers determining what the world thought about him.

Before the news conference, however, Arthur wanted to let certain people know what was coming. The night before, he called his immediate family first. They knew he had AIDS, but he wanted to let them know he was going to tell the world. Calls were made to his brother Johnnie, his stepmother, and his stepsister and stepbrother, as well as to members of Jeanne's family. Arthur also called the secretary of health and human services, Dr. Louis Sullivan. Dr. Sullivan, a distinguished African American medical doctor, was a close friend of Arthur's and a member of President George H. W. Bush's cabinet. Arthur asked Dr. Sullivan to pass the news to the first lady, Barbara Bush. Arthur had voted for George Bush in 1988 and was fond of the Bush family. He thought the president and the first lady should be among those who knew in advance what was coming. Arthur was especially surprised and grateful to receive a phone call from President Bush himself after Dr. Sullivan had alerted the Bush family. The president wished Arthur and his family well and said they would be in his prayers. Arthur also called his friend and financial adviser, Donald Dell, who said he would be at the news conference to lend Arthur support.

Arthur next turned to HBO, the cable network, for assistance with the news conference. Among his many broadcasting duties was serving as an HBO commentator for tennis events. The network agreed immediately to set up the conference at their headquarters in New York City and to alert the sports media. To assist him in drafting his statement, Arthur called on Frank Deford, a sports journalist and writer for *Newsweek* magazine and a trusted friend who had worked with him on his book *Arthur Ashe—Portrait in Motion: A Diary.*

The dreaded moment arrived. It was April 8, 1992. Arthur and Jeanne went to the HBO office in Manhattan for the 3:30 P.M. news conference. Arthur began reading from his prepared statement, outlining his health problems leading up to the fateful transfusion in 1983. He confirmed that it was indeed true that he had AIDS. He also vented his anger at having to reveal his condition. "There was certainly no compelling medical or physical necessity to go public with my medical condition," he said. Toward the end of his statement, as he thought of Camera, Arthur became so overwhelmed with emotion that he could not continue. Jeanne stepped up to the microphone and finished reading his remarks.[2]

After going public, Arthur had hoped he would feel a sense of relief. At last the secret was no more. But he didn't. His emotions were mixed. He was still very angry that he could not have the right to privacy that other people might enjoy under these circumstances. He also felt some guilt. He knew that guilt about having contracted the illness was pointless. He had gotten AIDS not because of his behavior but because of bad luck. Some readers wrote to USA Today and supported Arthur's right to privacy. Others, however, felt that if he had gone public earlier, he might have helped some people avoid getting the disease. This kind of guilt, however, was also pointless. He had lived his life the best he could according to the principles and ethics he believed in, as he always did. He could not turn back the clock and redo things. In any event, his whole purpose now was to look forward. Since his AIDS was no longer a secret, it quickly dawned on Arthur that he could devote his remaining time to fighting the disease and educating people about this deadly illness.

SPEAKING OUT FOR HIS BELIEFS

Immediately after his announcement, Arthur plunged into a round of activities, many now focused on his mission to speak out on AIDS. His other interests, however, were not put aside. April 1992 was the month he founded the African American Athletic Association (AAAA), with its goal of mentoring black student athletes and improving their academic performance. Also in April, he received an honorary degree from Kalamazoo College in Michigan, where he had played many matches as a junior player. Other honorary degrees followed later in 1992, and on each occasion, Arthur spoke about AIDS, shining the light on a subject that many people continued to find uncomfortable and frightening. He also spoke to high school students and to professional associations such as the National Press Club in Washington, D.C. His other responsibilities to such organizations as Aetna, Head USA, ABC-TV, and HBO continued without a break. He would not let up the pace. For Arthur, who was not sure how long he had, it was essential to talk about AIDS and to fulfill his obligations as long as he could.

In June, Arthur, Jeanne, and Camera took a brief break and went to Wimbledon. It was a working vacation of sorts, because Arthur was serving as a commentator on the tournament for HBO. During some time off from his work, Arthur took Camera on a nostalgic and emotional stroll around the courts, showing her where he had won his 1975 singles title. Although she was too young to fully understand what he was saying, for Arthur it was a wonderful moment to be walking around Wimbledon, holding the hand of his little girl and visiting the site of one of his greatest tennis triumphs. He returned to the United States feeling refreshed and optimistic. By early summer, Arthur was enjoying playing golf at the Sleepy Hollow Country Club near New York City. Arthur had discovered that golf was one of his great joys, not only a wonderful way to get out in the open and exercise, but an excellent way to relax from his hectic schedule.

Soon after his announcement, Arthur decided that he wanted to do something more concrete to fight AIDS than simply to speak out on the subject before select audiences. In August, he announced the creation of the Arthur Ashe Foundation to Defeat AIDS. Arthur was acutely aware that AIDS knew no national boundaries, and as bad as the epidemic was in the United States, it was worse in places such as Africa. Especially hard hit was Central Africa, where nations such as Uganda, the Central African Republic, and Zaïre (now the Democratic Republic of the Congo) were being devastated by AIDS. Accordingly, Arthur decided that about half of the money raised by his foundation would be used to fund the research and treatment of AIDS outside the United States.

In September, a tennis exhibition to raise money for AIDS research was held at Flushing Meadows in New York, the site of the U.S. Open. Arthur was particularly happy to receive a check for $114,000 from the USTA, money raised at the exhibition. Shortly after this event, Arthur received a phone call from his old friend Randall Robinson, the head of TransAfrica. Robinson told Arthur that TransAfrica and the NAACP had made a decision to picket the White House to protest the Bush administration's policy toward refugees from Haiti. Arthur immediately agreed to join the demonstration. He had been deeply disturbed by the plight of the Haitian refugees. Because of political unrest in Haiti, thousands of refugees in small, unsafe boats had taken to sea in an effort to reach the United States. The policy of the Bush administration was that these people were not really political refugees entitled to asylum in the

United States, but that they were leaving Haiti for economic reasons. Economic refugees were not entitled to asylum under the law and could be turned back to their home country. Dozens had drowned in their efforts to reach Florida, and those being turned back, Arthur believed, faced an uncertain and dangerous future—imprisonment or perhaps even execution at the hands of the repressive Haitian government.

The protest at the White House, on September 9, 1992, was intended to highlight the hypocrisy of the U.S. position. Refugees from the Communist dictatorship of Fidel Castro in Cuba were welcomed to the United States with open arms. The Cubans were politically powerful in Florida, where many thousands had migrated, fleeing Castro in the early 1960s. The Haitians, who were black, were not. They were poor and had no political voice in the U.S. administration to fight for them. The problem, Arthur believed, was a double standard because of race. Arthur was well aware that the protest at the White House would be illegal, because it is unlawful for groups to picket within a certain distance of the White House. He also did not relish protesting against the administration of President Bush, whom he liked and admired and who had been so kind to him when he went public with his AIDS announcement. Nevertheless, Arthur felt that the principles involved in this issue went beyond personalities.

The organizers of the demonstration planned it carefully and informed the police in advance, and the police were out in force to arrest the demonstrators. Arthur did not welcome the prospect of being arrested. He thought of his father, who supported the civil rights movement but had always been uneasy about civil disobedience and anything that would lead to breaking the law, no matter how minor the offense. In a way, Arthur was glad his father did not have to see him on this day: He was one of those arrested. He was handcuffed and taken to the police station, where he paid a $50 fine, then went to the airport and returned to New York. This demonstration was important, in his mind, because it united African Americans and Haitians—two groups who normally did not mix or even get along despite their racial similarities—in a common goal for justice. He had come a long way from the young man who was taught to behave himself and never to challenge a linesman's call in a tennis match.

The day after returning from Washington, Arthur began to experience chest pains. He went immediately to the hospital, where tests showed that he had suffered another heart attack. The only good news was that the attack was minor and that his heart had not suffered any further damage. But this latest setback helped Arthur focus on the wider issue of health care in the United States. He had money and was able to afford the thousands of dollars a year he had to pay out of pocket for the many medications he had to take. But what about poor people? Or people who were out of work? Or families headed by single parents? What were they to do when they were struck by serious illness? Health care was emerging as a major issue in the presidential campaign of 1992 in which the incumbent Republican president, George H. W. Bush, faced his Democratic opponent, Governor Bill Clinton of Arkansas.

After some thought, Arthur agreed to have his name put on an initiative aimed at finding innovative solutions to the health care problems of people living in Brooklyn, New York, and in urban areas across the country. In December 1992 the Arthur Ashe Institute for Urban Health at the Health Science Center of the State University of New York in Brooklyn was launched. Arthur agreed to serve as the first chairman of the board. Arthur toured a ward at the center that was filled with children suffering from AIDS. He was deeply moved by their plight, and he made sure that they knew that he, too, had the disease they were fighting. Arthur felt it was important for him to visit other hospitals that treated children with AIDS. He wanted the world to know that the disease was not restricted to adults, but that many young people were among those stricken with the ailment. Some had gotten the ailment through blood transfusions, while others, the children of drug abusers with AIDS, had been born with the disease.

Since his announcement in April 1992, Arthur had maintained a hectic schedule, fulfilling his long-standing obligations and taking on new responsibilities speaking out on the subject of AIDS and setting in motion concrete steps to help fight the disease. At Christmas, he and his family would be heading off to Florida, where they hoped to relax for the holiday.

It was a tradition for Arthur to conduct a tennis clinic at the Doral over the Christmas season. Arthur was in an upbeat mood for the holiday. That month, the magazine *Sports Illustrated* had named him "Sportsman of the Year," an award that gave him great satisfaction. On December 21, Camera celebrated her birthday at a festive party that Arthur videotaped. The family then left the frigid weather of New York behind and flew to Florida.

Arthur was looking forward to the tennis clinic and to getting in some golf. It was while playing a round of gold with Jeanne's father, John Moutoussamy, that Arthur first noticed he was having some difficulty breathing. He was baffled by this development, since he had not been exerting himself all that much, but since he was a heart patient, he naturally thought of a heart problem first before anything else. After calling his doctor in New York, Arthur went to see Dr. Michael Collins at Miami Baptist Hospital. Dr. Collins had been one of the first doctors Arthur had seen in New York in 1979 when he had his heart attack. Dr. Collins performed a number of tests and could not find any problem with Arthur's heart. He thought the shortness of breath might be a lung problem. A chest X-ray, however, did not show anything wrong.

PNEUMONIA

The coughing and shortness of breath continued. On New Year's Eve, December 31, 1992, Arthur played another round of golf, but with increasing difficulty. In addition, he began to experience pains in his chest—always the most serious warning for a heart patient—and he noticed that he had pain simply when he inhaled, a deep pain that gripped his chest when he breathed in. New Year's Eve was spent with Jeanne's parents and her brother Claude and his wife, but Arthur and Jeanne did not stay to welcome in 1993. Noticing that Arthur was having increasing problems breathing, Jeanne suggested that they fly back to New York the following day. They left early to arrange a flight. In their home, Camera watched the ball come down in Times Square in New York as Jeanne made phone calls to finalize their reservations.

The following morning, January 1, 1993, Arthur awakened with a fever of almost 102 degrees. Coughing and in pain, he took over-the-counter medications purchased in a drug store, and that helped bring down his temperature enough that he could travel. The family flew to New York from Miami and went immediately to New York Hospital, where they were met by Dr. Henry Murray. Dr. Murray put Arthur immediately on a powerful antibiotic, but it had no effect. Arthur was forced to undergo an extremely unpleasant procedure called a bronchoscopy, in which a tube is inserted in your nose and forced down through your throat into your lungs. At the end of the tube is a small camera that can examine a patient's lung tissue up close.

After the 40-minute procedure, the doctors had a diagnosis. Arthur was suffering from *Pneumocytis carinii* pneumonia (PCP), a rare infection of the lungs that often strikes AIDS patients. PCP had been found before the AIDS era in poor people in Eastern Europe, people who because of poverty and poor health had weak immune systems. Thus far during his years with AIDS, Arthur had suffered from only two of the common infections that hit people with AIDS: toxoplasmosis, and now PCP.

The treatment for PCP was a drug called pentamidine, which Arthur had been inhaling in aerosol form for years as a preventive measure. Now that he had a case of PCP, he was given the drug intravenously.

As he waited for it to take effect, he shivered and sweated under heavy blankets. Arthur was able to tolerate the pentamidine fairly well, although it was known at times to interfere with the heart's electrical impulses. Eventually, it did its work, and Arthur's fever and cough began to improve. But he was weakened by the attack. As with AZT, pentamidine was an early AIDS treatment that was often as toxic as the disease itself. There were few options when it came to treating PCP, and this powerful drug was often the only choice, despite its powerful side effects.

As he began to recover slowly, Arthur noticed that he was in a very nice room—more hotel- than hospital-like, it had beautiful wooden floors, nice furniture (except for the standard-issue metal hospital bed), and looked out over the beautiful Manhattan skyline. One of his doctor's told Arthur that in this very room back in the 1950s, then-Senator John F. Kennedy (who became president of the United States in 1961) had stayed as a patient. Arthur reflected on the coincidences of life. President Kennedy was someone he admired. Now here he was a patient in the same room the late president had once occupied.

As he improved, Arthur thought more about Haiti. He talked with Randall Robinson, and they both agreed that more action would be needed to keep this issue in the news. Arthur was also grateful to receive an invitation to the inauguration of President Bill Clinton in Washington on January 20, 1993. Although he had supported George Bush in 1988, in 1992 Arthur voted for his opponent, Bill Clinton. Although he remained fond of President Bush, Arthur liked Clinton's positions on many issues, especially his desire to overhaul the American health care system to make sure than no one went without health insurance.

As the days wore on, Arthur reflected on his life, on how fortunate he had been despite his illnesses. He took great solace in reading the Bible and in listening to classical music. And he thought how blessed he had been to have a wonderful family like Jeanne and Camera. He was able to call people and to do more work on his autobiography, *Days of Grace*.

Arthur was released from the hospital on January 18, 1993. But he had to return. AIDS is a disease that can work slowly, or it can take its victims quickly. It took Arthur quickly. Arthur was feeling optimistic enough to plan a father-daughter dance for Valentine's Day, February 14. It was not to be. The pneumonia returned more fiercely than before. On February 2, Arthur returned to New York Hospital. His breathing had gotten so bad that he was put on a ventilator, a machine that helps a person breathe. For the next four days he struggled against the infection, but his body became weaker and weaker and in the end was no longer able to fight back. The medical staff heroically labored in vain to save his life. A little after 3 P.M. on February 6, 1993, Arthur Ashe died. He was 49 years old. In the hall outside his room, Jeanne had kept vigil. The doctors came out of his room and told her that they had been unable to save him. Jeanne had been a realist over the years. She knew that this day might come, that in fact, it was likely to come. Still, the news was devastating.

After composing herself, Jeanne went home and braced herself for the most difficult thing she would ever have to do: tell Camera that her daddy was not coming home from the hospital. Friends began to gather in the Ashe's apartment, despite the difficulty of travel. Outside, a blizzard gripped New York. Camera at first did not react outwardly to the news, a behavior not uncommon in children her age. Later, she would ask questions, and Jeanne would answer them as well as she could. It took time for the news to sink into Camera's young mind.

When he died, Arthur Ashe was still a young man, but the world had been greatly blessed by his presence.

NOTES

1. The full extent of Arthur's rage can be seen in the fact that the entire first chapter of his autobiography is devoted to his AIDS announcement. See *Days of Grace*, pp. 1–34. The chapter is entitled "My Outing," a term normally used to describe the involuntary malevolent exposure of a person's homosexuality.

2. For a more detailed summary of his remarks to the press, see ibid., pp. 15–16.

Chapter 9

THE LEGACY OF ARTHUR ASHE

How should we remember Arthur Ashe? Why should we think about him and appreciate his life so many years after he died? As the years have passed since his death, he has remained a strong memory in the world of tennis, a man whose career and life are revered and honored by millions of people. But the legacy of Arthur Ashe does not rest in one kind of achievement. Had he been solely a tennis player who disappeared after his retirement, or who spent his retirement uninvolved in public issues, he would undoubtedly still be remembered as an outstanding athlete and the first male African American to break racial barriers in tennis and win Grand Slam titles—especially Wimbledon. He would not have been considered the most powerful player (like a McEnroe or a Connors in the 1970s or an Andy Roddick, with his 150-mile-per-hour serve, in the early 2000s). Nor would he have been remembered for the number of titles he won (Martina Navratilova, the great Czech-born champion, won nine Wimbledon singles titles compared with Arthur's one). Nor would he have been remembered for the longevity of his career (Navratilova continued to play tennis into her late 40s, whereas ill health cut Arthur's competitive years short when he was in his mid-30s).

But his life did not end when the game of tennis ended for him. He kept his hand in tennis by taking on the challenging—some would say impossible—job of being captain of the U.S. Davis Cup team at a time when talented but difficult-to-manage young players were making their mark in the world of tennis. But more important, he went on to become an activist and a spokesman for causes that he felt deeply about: apartheid, health care for the poor, educational excellence for African

American athletes, and the plight of Haitian refugees, to name just a few. And here he put his body on the line, willing to risk arrest and negative publicity to speak out on issues he believed passionately in.

And then there was AIDS. In the face of a fatal illness, he persevered and, when he was forced to go public with the information about his illness, he became an activist and spokesman for all people who suffered from this dreaded disease. His trademark as a tennis player had always been his grace and dignity, especially when under pressure. Arthur Ashe the athlete almost never lost his cool. Even when faced with managing difficult young players as captain of the Davis Cup team, he almost always remained calm and reasonable. Arthur Ashe the activist and humanitarian kept his focus on the issues that deeply moved him. And in the end, Arthur Ashe the patient brought to his illness the same grace, dignity, and coolness under pressure that had characterized his earlier life.

The world mourned his passing. It was difficult to believe that he was gone. Less than a year had passed since his announcement of his illness. It was hard to believe that this young man—so smart, so attractive, who had a beautiful wife and child—was no longer with us. His body was taken from New York to the state of his birth, where he lay in state in the Executive Mansion of Virginia, in Richmond. The little boy who in life had been denied access to white-only playgrounds was honored in death in the governor's mansion of the state of Virginia. More than 5,400 people walked past the casket to pay tribute to Arthur. The next day, on February 10, 1993, his body was laid to rest in Richmond. Some 6,500 people attended the funeral service, including the Rev. Andrew Young, who had married Jeanne and Arthur in 1977, the Rev. Jesse Jackson, Gov. L. Douglas Wilder of Virginia, and Mayor David Dinkins of New York, that city's first African American mayor.[1] Arthur was remembered around the world in newspaper editorials and in eulogies from church pulpits. He had touched people beyond the borders of the United States, especially in countries such as South Africa and Haiti, where he had raised his voice to bring justice to their peoples.

Inevitably, the time came when people began speaking of some sort of permanent memorial to honor Arthur. In Richmond, a movement was begun to have a statue of Arthur placed on Monument Avenue. This thoroughfare, one of the main streets of the city, is so named because it contains numerous statues, most of them monuments that honor famous leaders of the Confederacy such as President (of the Confederacy) Jefferson Davis, and generals Robert E. Lee and Stonewall Jackson. Some white people were not happy about having Arthur Ashe—an African American athlete who had died of AIDS—placed side by side with the venerable leaders of the Confederate States of America, the very government that had tried to perpetuate slavery in the 1860s. And some black leaders were also upset at the prospect of a statue honoring Arthur being placed on Monument Avenue, so rich in its associations to the Confederacy. His statue, they believed, did not belong side by side with the men who had fought so hard to keep black people enslaved.

In the end, the project went forward. The statue is situated on the corner of Roseneath and Monument Avenues. Jeanne Ashe was one of those who did not want to the statue to be situated on Monument Avenue, and when the day of its dedication came, on July 10, 1996, on what would have been Arthur's 53rd birthday, she did not attend the ceremonies, in order to express her opposition. From her point of view, a more appropriate location would have been before a planned hall of fame dedicated to the African American athlete. Despite the controversy, the statue went up, where it stands today, the lone black man among a procession of white slave owners who lived more than a century ago. But the Arthur Ashe statue is different in style and content. A 12-foot-high bronze statue of Arthur stands atop a 44-ton granite base. It shows Arthur holding a tennis racket in one hand and books in the other. Statues of four children sitting at his feet gaze up at him from below, as if he is teaching them and showing them the way. The tennis racket and the books are appropriate symbols of two things that meant so much to him in his life: tennis and education. At the base of the statue is a biblical inscription that reads, "Since we are surrounded by so great a cloud of witnesses, let us lay aside every weight, and the sin which so easily ensnares us, and let us run with endurance the race that is set before us" (Hebrews 12: 1–3).

The entire memorial, which quickly became a popular tourist attraction, summarizes much about Arthur—his greatness as a tennis player, his love of learning, and his commitment to children. Over the years, people have continued to express reservations about the statue and its location. Some writers have called it an ugly statue, while others in Richmond are still clearly unhappy that a black man stands on this stretch of land in Richmond. Nevertheless, the Arthur Ashe memorial has now become a fixture on Monument Avenue, a lone African American standing amidst a procession of Confederate figures.[2]

Another honor was bestowed in Arthur's memory in 1997. The USTA announced in February of that year that it was naming its new stadium at the National Tennis Center in Flushing Meadows, Queens, The Arthur Ashe Stadium. This was an honor that Jeanne felt was appropriate, and she proudly attended the news conference at which USTA president Harry Marmion said "We are naming our new stadium in his honor because Arthur Ashe was the finest human being the sport of tennis has ever known."[3]

The first U.S. Open to be played at the new Arthur Ashe Stadium was in September 1997. The new arena, which cost $254 million to construct, towered over the nearby Louis Armstrong Stadium, where the U.S. Open had been played from 1978 to 1996. When Arthur won the first U.S. Open in 1968, the tournament was played in Forest Hills, at the West Side Tennis Club. Now, when spectators come to the most prestigious tournament in the United States, they enter a stadium that bears Arthur's name and are reminded that his presence graced the world of tennis for all too short a period.

For Jeanne and Camera, life went on. Jeanne continued her work as a photographer, taking special pleasure in using the Hasselbad camera Arthur gave to her on their last Christmas together in 1992. She has since published a number of distinguished works of photography.

The memory of Arthur Ashe is that of a multitalented man, a great athlete and humanitarian, and a great American. He was a champion on the court and a champion of human rights, and that made him a superb human being whose life is justly remembered and honored.

NOTES

1. "Slow Train to Eminence," *Sports Illustrated,* September 19, 1994.

2. Garber, Greg, "Ashe's Activism Helped Mold the Future," ESPN.com, February 6, 2003.

3. CNN.com.

APPENDIX A

GLOSSARY OF TENNIS TERMS

Below is a short list of terms that are used in the game of tennis. When one goes to a tennis match or watches one on television, these terms are likely to be heard, whether called out by linesmen or spoken by TV commentators.

Backhand   A stroke made by holding the racket with the back of the hand facing the direction that the ball is hit in.

Baseline   The boundary line at either end of the tennis court.

Deuce   A term used to mean a tie in which each player has achieved 40 points. After a game has reached deuce, two consecutive points are needed by a player to win the game.

Forehand   A stroke made by holding the racket with the palm of the hand facing the direction that the ball is hit in.

Grand Slam   A term used to refer to the four most prestigious tournaments in tennis: Wimbledon, the U.S. Open, the French Open, and the Australian Open. If a player wins all four in a year, he or she is said to have won "the Grand Slam."

Ground stroke   A stroke made by hitting a ball that has rebounded from the ground.

Lawn Tennis   An early term used to describe the game of tennis, which was played on courts made of grass.

Love   In tennis scoring, the term used to mean "zero," For example, the score 15-love means 15–0.

Match   A tennis competition won when a player wins a specified number of sets.

Set   A division of a tennis match that is won when a player wins at least six games, defeating an opponent by two games or in a tiebreaker.

Serve   The first swing of the racket that puts the ball into play.

Service line   A line parallel to the net behind which the player stands to make a serve.

APPENDIX B

ARTHUR ASHE'S GRAND SLAM RECORD, 1968–1979

From the beginning of the open era in tennis, Arthur Ashe played for eleven years in the Grand Slam tournaments: The U.S. Open, the Australian Open, the French Open, and Wimbledon. Except for two occasions (1970 and 1978), he never played in all four tournaments in one year, but he always managed to play in at least one. He won the singles titles in three Grand Slam events: The U.S. Open (1968), the Australian Open (1970), and Wimbledon (1975).

Year	U.S. Open	Australian Open	French Open	Wimbledon
1968	WON	—	—	SF
1969	SF	—	4th round	SF
1970	QF	WON	QF	4th round
1971	SF	F	QF	3rd round
1972	F	—	—	—
1973	3rd round	—	4th round	—
1974	QF	—	4th round	3rd round
1975	4th round	—	—	WON
1976	2nd round	—	4th round	4th round
1977	—	QF	—	—

(Continued)

(*Continued*)

Year	U.S. Open	Australian Open	French Open	Wimbledon
1978	4th round	SF	4th round	1st round
1979	—	—	3rd round	1st round

Symbols used in table:
QF (means Arthur reached the quarterfinals)
SF (means Arthur reached the semifinals)
F (means Arthur reached the finals)
2nd, 3rd, and 4th rounds (means Arthur reached these rounds before being eliminated)
No symbol means Arthur did not play in the tournament that year.

APPENDIX C

ARTHUR ASHE'S AWARDS AND HONORS

Honorary degrees:

Bryan College
Dartmouth College
LeMoyne-Owen College
Long Island University
Princeton University
Saint John's University
Trinity University
Hartford College
Virginia Union University
University of South Carolina

Winner of 1964 Johnston Award, prestigious honor awarded annually to the American tennis player who contributes the most to the growth of the sport while exhibiting good sportsmanship and character

Elected president of Association of Tennis Professionals (ATP) in 1974

Inducted into International Tennis Hall of Fame (1985)

Inducted into the Tennis Hall of Fame (1985)

Named *Sport Illustrated* Sportsman of the Year (1992)

Medal of Freedom (posthumously awarded by President Bill Clinton)

Olympic Order (posthumously awarded)

APPENDIX D

NOTABLE AFRICAN AMERICANS IN TENNIS

Arthur Ashe achieved worldwide fame in a tennis world that was changing rapidly. The tennis that was covered by the sports press was the white tennis world. He was able to break into that world and dominate the game for a period by his sheer skill but also by his ability to get along with all kinds of people and in all kinds of situations. He drew attention because of his game, but also because of the strength of his character and the nobility of the causes he championed.

But there were other African Americans who excelled in the world of tennis—some even in the world of black tennis only. With few exceptions, the blacks who played before Arthur did not break into the white tennis world, nor did they necessarily even achieve much notoriety in the world of black sports fans in general, who tended to remain fixated on football, basketball, and baseball. Yet, their contributions and skills did much to prepare the way for Arthur Ashe. Below is a short list of some of the black tennis players who preceded Arthur Ashe, as well as a few notable players who came after him. There were others, many of whom are not well known today, but who nevertheless contributed to keeping tennis alive among African Americans.

Althea Gibson: Althea Gibson, like Arthur Ashe, was born in Virginia and trained with Dr. Johnson. In 1950, she became the first African American allowed to enter the national championships conducted by the U.S. Lawn Tennis Association (USLTA). In 1956, with her victory in the French national tournament, she became the first African American to win a Grand Slam title. In 1957 and 1958 she won the Wimbledon crown, becoming the first African American to capture that title. After retiring from tennis, she played golf as a member of the Ladies Professional Golf Association. Althea Gibson is considered one of the all-time greats in twentieth-century tennis history.

Robert Ryland: Robert Ryland grew up in Chicago and played tennis in high school. In 1939, he won the junior championship of the American Tennis Association (ATA). He was the first African American to play in the National Collegiate Athletic Association (NCAA) tennis tournament and the first to play as a student at Wayne University (now Wayne State University), Michigan, after enrolling there in 1945. After retiring from active play, he became a well-known coach to celebrities, including Bill Cosby, Dustin Hoffman, and Robert MacNamara, among many others.

Zina Garrison: Zina Garrison was a player whose career in the 1980s and 1990s led to 14 singles titles. Although she never won a Grand Slam title, she enjoyed the distinction of reaching the finals at Wimbledon in 1990, the first African American woman to get that far since Althea Gibson in 1958. She won a silver medal at the Seoul Olympics in 1988 playing doubles with Pam Shriver.

Oscar Johnson: Oscar Johnson was the first black tennis player to win an integrated championship match when he captured the National Public Parks Junior Championship in 1948. He thus became the first African American to enter and win a USLTA-sanctioned tournament.

Ora Mae Washington: Ora Mae Washington was a black woman tennis player who won the ATA women's singles titles from 1929 to 1937. After the end of her career as a player, she became a basketball coach.

Marie Ross: Marie Ross won three women's singles and one women's doubles championships in matches held in Kansas City, Missouri, in the 1940s.

Mary Etta Fine and Eva Belle Fine: Even before the Williams sisters, Mary Etta Fine and her sister, Eva Belle Fine, played tennis. They won the women's doubles championship at Wilberforce University, Xenia, Ohio, in 1957.

Serena Williams and Venus Williams: Perhaps among the most famous athletes of all time, the Williams sisters rose from the obscurity of their neighborhood in Los Angeles to the peak of the tennis world, winning Grand Slam titles and other matches around the world. The tennis world encouraged a rivalry between the sisters, which the two seemed more than willing to play into, although they seemed devoted to each other as sisters. They competed against each other in a number of Grand Slam titles, including Wimbledon and the U.S. Open. After a period that saw the older sister, Venus, triumphant, the younger Serena began to dominate their matches.

BIBLIOGRAPHY

WORKS BY ARTHUR ASHE

Arthur's monumental three-volume history of the black athlete in America was published in 1988:

Ashe, Jr., Arthur R. *A Hard Road to Glory: A History of the African-American Athlete, Volume I: 1619–1918*. New York: Warner Books, 1988.

———. *A Hard Road to Glory: A History of the African-American Athlete, Volume II: 1919–1945*. New York: Warner Books, 1988.

———. *A Hard Road to Glory: A History of the African-American Athlete, Volume III: Since 1946*. New York: Warner Books, 1988.

Ashe, Arthur, and Arnold Rampersad. *Day of Grace: A Memoir*. New York: Ballantine, 1993. Arthur worked on this memoir in the final months of his life. He discusses his youth, his career in tennis, and his life after his playing career ended.

Ashe, Arthur, and Frank Deford. *Arthur Ashe—Portrait in Motion: A Diary*. New York: Carroll & Graf, 1975. This work is essentially a diary of Arthur's life in the year 1973, which included his famous visit to South Africa and the beginnings of his fight against apartheid.

WORKS ABOUT ARTHUR ASHE

Collins, Bud. *Total Tennis: The Ultimate Tennis Encyclopedia*, 3rd ed. Toronto: Sportsclassic Books, 2003. An excellent general reference work that contains a detailed chronology of tennis history, biographies of noted tennis players, and descriptions of famous matches and tournaments. Collins is a tennis commentator and an expert on the sport.

Garber, Greg. "Ashe's Activism Helped Mold the Future," ESPN.com, February 6, 2003.

————. "Those Ashe Touched Carry on His Work," ESPN.com, February 6, 2004.

"He Did All He Could," *Sports Illustrated*, February 15, 1993.

Lutz, Francis Earle. *Richmond in World War II*. Richmond, VA: Dietz Press, 1951. A history of Virginia's capital city during the early 1940s, this book gives a sense of what it was like to live in the South during these years. Although segregation was still in full force, African Americans are acknowledged in the book.

Martin, Marvin. *Arthur Ashe: of Tennis and the Human Spirit*. Danbury, CT: Franklin Watts, 1999.

Moutoussamy-Ashe, Jeanne. *Daddy and Me*. New York: Knopf, 1993. A picture book that documents Arthur's touching relationship with Camera. Photographs were all taken by Jeanne and include memorable shots of Arthur and Camera at home in the final years and months of his life.

Randolph, Laura B., "Jeanne Moutoussamy-Ashe: On Love, Loss, and Life after Arthur," *Ebony*, October 1993.

"Slow Train to Eminence," *Sports Illustrated*, September 19, 1994.

Towle, Mike, *I Remember Arthur Ashe: Memories of a True Tennis Pioneer and Champion of Social Causes by the People Who Knew Him* (Nashville, TN: Cumberland House, 2001). A collection of remembrances of Arthur by people who knew him from his days in Richmond to the end of his life. An excellent source for appreciating how Arthur affected the many people who came into his life.

WEB SITES

http://www.daviscup.com is an excellent source for everything about Davis Cup play, including its history and the rules of the competition.

http://www.arthurasheinstitute.org is the Web site of the Arthur Ashe Institute for Urban Health, an organization he founded in December 1992, just two months before his death.

http://www.cmgww.com/sports/Ashe is described as the "official Arthur Ashe Web site." It is a good place to start research on Ashe since it contains photographs, bibliographies, and information about his career and life.

INDEX

About the Author

RICHARD STEINS is a freelance writer and editor who has written numerous books for young readers. Among his recent publications is *Colin Powell: A Biography* (Greenwood, 2003).